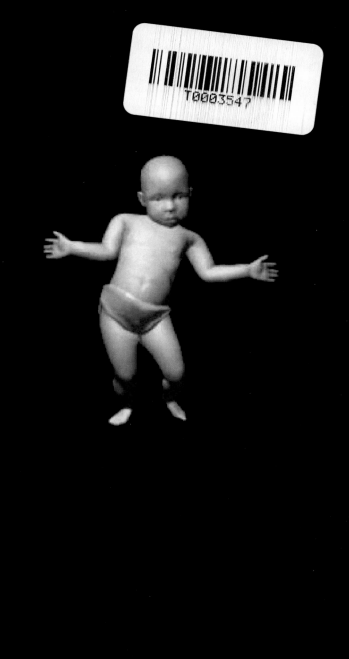

are we human?

notes on an archaeology
of design

by

Beatriz Colomina
& Mark Wigley

Lars Müller Publishers

The question *are we human?* is both urgent and ancient. It might even be the oldest question of all – reverberating through the ages from the smallest gestures of daily life to the largest transformations of technology, biology, and geology. Perhaps the human is simply the species that asks this of itself. But other animals might have doubts about their identity too. Our species might not be as unique as it thinks or hopes. Even a machine might ask itself if it is human and some machines may well be more human than people. The question *are we human?* is from the beginning a hesitation about the relationship between ourselves and everything around or inside us. These notes dive into that hesitation to explore the intimate relationship between design and human. They are field notes from a continuous stream of conversations, classes, symposia, readings, interviews, site visits, meetings, walks, and meals during the last year and a half as we prepared the 3rd Istanbul Design Biennial. The evolving overlapping thoughts don't provide answers to the question that defines our species. This is not a design guide or a do-it-yourself humanity manual. No reason to think it will change you. The notes just try consider the role of design in defining the human animal. If the human is a question mark, design is the way that question is engaged. An archaeology of design is an archaeology of curiosity.

1

THE MIRROR
OF DESIGN

Design always presents itself as serving the human but its real ambition is to redesign the human.

The history of design is therefore a history of evolving conceptions of the human. To talk about design is to talk about the state of our species.

Humans have always been radically reshaped by the designs they produce and the world of design keeps expanding. We live in a time when everything is designed, from our carefully crafted individual looks and online identities to the surrounding galaxies of personal devices, new materials, interfaces, networks, systems, infrastructures, data, chemicals, organisms, and genetic codes. The average day involves the experience of thousands of layers of design that reach deep into the ground and outer space but also deep into our bodies and brains. We literally live inside design, like the spider lives inside the web constructed from inside its own body. But unlike the spider, we have spawned countless overlapping and interacting webs. Even the planet itself has been completely encrusted by design as a geological layer. There is no longer an outside to the world of design. Design has become the world.

Design is what you are standing on. It is what holds you up. And every layer of design rests on another and another and another. To think about design demands an archaeological approach. You have to dig. Dig into the ground, underground, beneath the seabed, and deep into the Earth. Dig into the things sitting on the ground – buildings, cities, treetops, and antennae. Dig over the ground – into the air, clouds, and outer space. Dig even into the invisible layers – data storage, formulas, protocols, circuits, spectra, chemical reactions, chemical reactions, gene sequences, and social media posts. Digging, documenting, dissecting, discussing – digging, that is, into ourselves.

If design needs archaeology, archaeology has always been about design. It reconstructs human activity by analyzing the material traces of technofossils. It treats every artifact and pattern it uncovers with a delicate brush or a penetrating X-ray as evidence of human life and intentions. Sedimented layers are painstakingly exposed to replay sequences of human sociality, mobility, diet, metabolism, symbolism, and mental capacity. This obsessive forensic analysis deploys the most precise measurements and carbon dating techniques. Yet the evidence is always partial and the analytical framework is never innocent. Archaeology is an amalgam of polemical speculative debate and the latest understanding of scientific rigor. It is a kind of reverse engineering of design. It tries to recover possible pasts while design looks forward to possible futures. Design is a form of projection, to shape something rather than find it, to invent something and think about the possible outcomes of that invention. This endless reshaping and speculation about possible outcomes is uniquely human. The archaeology of design is not simply about the history of the human animal as revealed in all the layers of artifacts. It uncovers the sedimented ways of reinventing the human.

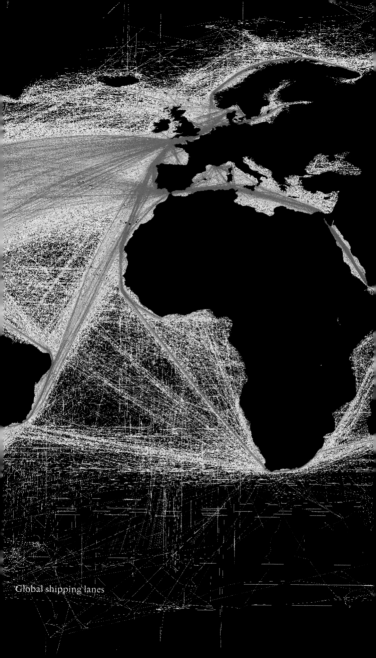

Global shipping lanes

Design is the most human thing about us. Design is what makes the human. It is the basis of social life, from the earliest artifacts to today's ongoing exponential expansion of human capability. The human radiates design in all directions. The imprint of the human is in the land, the oceans, the atmosphere, the plants, animals, organisms of every kind, chemicals, genetic makeup, and all frequencies of the mainly invisible electromagnetic spectrum. There is no water whose temperature, movement, and chemistry has not been affected. No air is unmarked. There is hardly any dimension of the natural world that has not been affected by human activity. Most of the Earth's surface has been massively transformed through urbanization and agriculture. There is an ever-accelerating reduction of biodiversity through the devastation of countless species through loss of habitat, overfishing and overhunting, industrial chemicals, pollution, and the invention of new species of plants and animals through selective breeding and genetic editing along with the acceleration of climate change driven by burning fossil fuels. The designs that mark human life are not just the cultural and technical artifacts that eventually

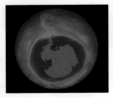 make their way into museums. They are the precarious movements of refugees, the collapse of biodiversity, the global flows of information and resources, the holes in the *ozone layer*←, the microplastic diffused throughout the oceans, the

radioactive isotopes from atomic testing in the atmosphere and the black carbon everywhere in the air and soil.

Humans no longer move across a small part of a very thin layer on the skin of the Earth, nomadically foraging for resources as if acting lightly on a vast stage. They now encircle the planet with layer upon layer of technocultural nets, posing an ever-greater threat to their own survival.

Midway Atoll, North Pacific
photo by Chris Jordan

The human might be the only species to have systematically designed its own extinction, and seems to be getting close to accomplishing the goal. Yet it largely acts as if it cannot do anything about it, staring at the prospect of its own demise as if transfixed, even with a lingering sense of pride in this massive self-destructive accomplishment. It is as if the image of a vast sublime natural world overwhelming the human attempt to comprehend it has been reversed. The human itself is now the overwhelming spectacle.

Enveloped in all the nets of its own making, the species constantly watches itself, as if fascinated by what it has become, increasingly aware that it is the very force that is making its own occupation of the planet, and that of most other species, ever more fragile. The human animal spends a remarkable amount of time looking at itself and its artifacts from an ever-increasing number of angles at every scale from the whole planet to atomic and now subatomic details. Conventional media channels provide continuous self-surveillance by bringing real-time images from every corner of the globe. The Internet offers multiple interfaces tracking the global movements of satellites, space junk, aircraft, ships, tweets, viruses, migration, and remittances. Millions of fixed webcams enable specific locations to be monitored from isolated stations in the Antarctic, desert highways, building sites, laboratories and apartments, to orbiting space stations. Instantly uploaded video from cellphones means the eyes with which we watch and are watched have multiplied exponentially. Live video feeds from cellphones in bedrooms, bathrooms, and battlefields have become the front lines of contemporary life. Once deeply private spaces are now accessible online. Personal actions and thoughts are experienced by global audiences. Individual movements, purchases, and communications are continuously detected, recorded, and analyzed throughout the day and night, as if constituting a massive collective selfie.

The transformative "blue marble" photograph of "our" planet taken on December 7, 1972, through the window of the Apollo 17 spacecraft as it headed toward the Moon – a singular, seemingly all-encompassing view of the "whole earth" from the outside with no visible human trace – has been displaced by live feeds from the International Space Station orbiting the planet at 17,000 miles an hour and countless views from the inside the Earth, as exemplified by the real-time images made, distributed, and watched on billions of cellphones. The technology to simultaneously visualize the Earth from outside and from inside is now in everybody's hands. Images and sounds from inside every dimension of human activity from the minutest scales of personal and chemical life to the widest expanses of inter-stellar space are gathered together in ever-shifting combi-nations on our small portable screens. Yet this real-time juxtaposition of multiple scales and angles does not form a seamless unity that either frightens or reassures. On the contrary, the image of our self-made habitat is a perma-nently changing mosaic. The new "whole earth" image is a real-time heterogeneous collage of collages that are riddled with questions. The unprecedented ability to collectively construct and share images does not mean that we all see the same thing. Our self-image is multiple and ever-shifting, as if we look into a vast multifaceted mirror in which the surfaces keep moving. We are fixated on a reflection that is as strange as hearing a recording of one's own voice, continually wondering what we are becoming. "Are we human?" is the most everyday question.

This huge and detailed self-portrait is full of gaps, technical limits, and multiple forms of censorship. It is paralleled by massive secretive surveillance systems with government, military, and corporations carrying out relentless visual and electronic tracking. The ability to see so much more is equally the ability to be seen much more. The human looks at itself looking at itself. Self-monitoring is a huge part of human activity — and is inseparable from design. The world of design is not the world of isolated artifacts seen in the spaces of design schools, exhibitions, museums, magazines, and stores or even in the wider spaces of the city or landscape. It is more in the planetary domain of overlapping geological and biological layers of artifacts at different scales and time frames and especially includes the ways that those layers are looked at, touched, and explored. Looking and grasping and reflecting is after all a key part of design. If design is basically a way of looking forward, this is not simply in the sense of inventing new artifacts. Artifacts become truly transformative by exceeding what was expected of them, exceeding our grasp. It is precisely in challenging us — triggering the potential of new ways of seeing, thinking, grasping, and acting — that design plays its role in redefining the human.

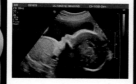

If you were coming to Earth from Mars it would be easy to observe that one species is entirely dominating the planet. But where would you meet this species? What would the first encounter be? Coming across a piece of space junk on the way in? Would you say, "Well, that's just a designed object and let me wait till I find out who made that." Or would your first thought be "Okay, contact with another creature"? After passing through clouds of satellites chirping to one another you would see airplanes and cities and sense the Internet buzzing with countless thoughts. Would you stop when you see organisms walking around on two legs and say "I found the humans"? Would you even see the fleshly bags of organs on your way into the crucial microbes, the proteins, or the genome of the creature? Or would you just pass the body by on the way into the electrical signals, the reshaped Earth, or the weather? You might conclude that this species dominating the planet emerged only 200,000 years ago, which is a pathetically short time, but this species is already like a kind of cloud of design, countless overlapping webs at the scale of the planet that are part of its body and brain. The human is occupying itself in a strange kind of way. It's fascinating but not clear if this species can survive itself, or even wants to. Better make some notes.

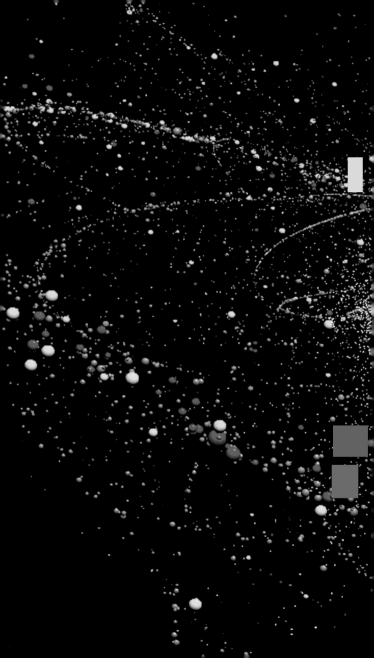

"It is time that we become human again..."

—Sigfried Giedion

2

THE PLASTIC
HUMAN

Human is an unstable category, even an
unstable being. It is not a clearly defined
biological organism with a particular form
and set of capacities that collaborates in
social networks to change things around it.

On the contrary, it is defined by its diversity and plasticity
– its ability to modify its own abilities. It is this very
plasticity, the radical instability of the human, that is
the basis of its massive impact. The more malleable and
indeterminate the species, the more extreme the impact.
In redesigning itself, it redesigns the planet. But equally
and simultaneously, the redesigned world redesigns the
designing animal. This is the real plasticity that is human.
The objects, networks, and systems are never simply
produced by a knowing subject dominating the material
world. Rather, a new kind of knowing and acting is made
possible by that adjusted world and is embedded in the
world itself. What makes the human human is not inside
the body or brain, or even inside the collective social body,
but in our interdependency with artifacts. The human is
suspended in a complex and continuous back and forth
between itself and artifacts, a flickering that ultimately
dissolves the distinction between them. Designed artifacts
have as much agency as the animal that seemingly

produced them. They transform the animal just as much as they are transformed by the animal. Or, to say it the other way around, the body and brain become artifacts. What is human is the radicality of this mutual exchange. The human is inseparable from the artifacts that it produces, with the human body having the extended shape of all the artifacts it has made and each artifact being an intimate part of its biology and brain. But also, and more important, the human emerges in the redefinition of capacity provided by the artifacts. In a sense, the artifacts are more human than the human.

Artifacts are therefore never simply the representatives of human intentions and abilities. They are also openings, possibilities of something new in the human, even a new human. There is always a gap between intentions and what is produced. The artifact offers something unexpected, some additional quality or resistance. This excess opens up new ways of thinking, new modes of design. It is not simply feedback to the makers. The network of people responsible for a particular artifact may not pick up on the potential opening. It might be taken advantage of by another group. The artifact may not have been intended in the first place or becomes transformative when used in ways that were not intended, when it breaks, or even when lost. It can do almost everything that was intended yet interact with other artifacts in unexpected ways to produce new potentials. Artifacts are always strange. They are never quite what we expect yet never simply outside us – even when they are appropriations from the outside world, like a rock or even a particular view, or the thought that something we come across is the artifact of another being. Artifacts are part of the body and brain. They are thoughts. But equally they are the potential of new ways of thinking.

In this sense, histories of the human are histories of artifacts and the interactivities between artifacts, seen as potentials rather than accomplishments, as if the Earth is a vast design studio in which human capacity is being tinkered with in unexpected ways. Artifacts are interfaces, enabling different forms of human engagement with the world but equally enabling the world to engage with the human differently. It's never simply human plus artifact plus Earth, with artifacts acting as interfaces between humans and between humans and the Earth. The human is both inseparable from "its" artifacts and challenged by them, and the Earth, understood as countless interacting life-forms, is also an active protagonist.

If the human is a designing animal and the Earth is its design studio, this animal is not a unique and distinct creature moving and thinking within that vast studio. The figure of the human is not sharply defined. It is part of the living Earth that it designs in just as the living Earth is part of it. The material world, whether the flows in a river valley or in the veins of our own bodies, is never just outside, waiting for human thought and action. It is precisely the lack of a clear line between human and world that provokes or energizes design as the attempt to draw such a line, our forever incomplete attempt to fashion a self-image and the forever unsatisfying attempt to come to terms with what we see in this continually reconstructed mirror.

The archaeology of design is not a self-congratulatory linear narrative about the steady evolution of a singular creature progressively adapting itself to the world with ever more sophisticated capacities and adapting to its own adaptions. Nor is it about the unevenness of such apparent progress with countless different directions, gaps, reversals, and loss of capacities. Rather, it is the history of a question mark.

From the moment we wake up in the morning, we are enveloped in design with our clothes, our shoes, the makeup we put on, our glasses, cell phones, furniture, appliances, computers, and even the paint on the walls surrounding us. This world of design extends out through the streets of the city across the countryside, over and under the oceans, into the atmosphere, and deep into outer space. *Voyager 1*, the spacecraft launched in 1977, is now beyond our solar system in interstellar space, travelling a million miles a day and continually reporting back. It is the piece of design that has reached the farthest away from us. Or, rather, we are stretching ourselves out by a million miles a day. Our eyes are now in interstellar space. In reverse, the world of design reaches deep into our bodies in a galaxy of chemicals and technologies. The artificial heart valve that has saved millions of lives since the early 1950s is like another satellite. This and countless other design innovations have doubled the average life expectancy over the last one hundred years. We are completely suspended in design.

"Nothing resembles
man less than a man."

–Balzac

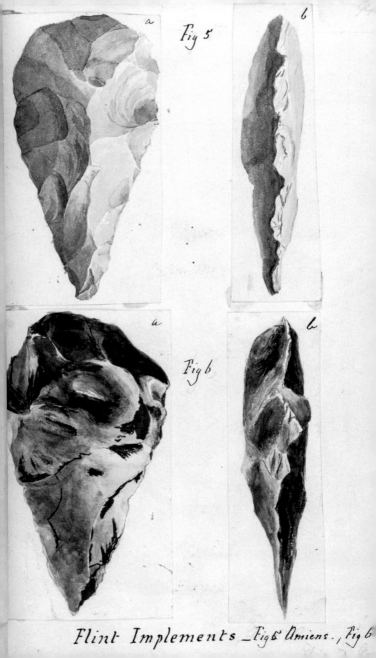

a   *Fig 5*   *b*

a   *Fig 6*   *b*

Flint Implements — Fig⁵ Amiens., Fig 6

3

BLOWS
OF DESIGN

Design can revolutionize thinking.
It's an immediate jolt, or one that
happens retroactively – years, even
hundreds of thousands of years,
later – like a time bomb.

On May 26 and June 2, 1859, geologist Joseph Prestwich
and archaeologist John Evans gave matching papers to
the scientific elite at the Royal Society and the Society of
Antiquaries in London. They asserted that some teardrop-
shaped stone objects found alongside the bones of long-
extinct mammals in digs in France and England exhibited
the uniquely human intelligence of design:

> That they really are implements fashioned by
> the hand of man, a single glance at a collection
> of them placed side by side, so as to show
> the analogy of form of the various specimens,
> would, I think, be sufficient to convince even
> the most skeptical. There is a uniformity of
> shape, a correctness of outline, and a sharpness
> about the cutting edges and points, which
> cannot be due to anything but design.[1]

The objects seem to have been systematically shaped by many blows with other stones to produce a thick round end and a thin sharp end. More impressively still, they are symmetrical along the axis from thick to thin and from front to back. The clarity and double symmetry of the shape, its repetition in hundreds of examples, and even the sense of shape gradually coming into focus with the traces of every chip on the surface of each object, was taken to be human. A kind of speculative picture of the early human started to be painted with just the evidence of this object whose visible design makes it an artifact "fashioned by the hand of man," in the mantra of Evans and Prestwich. It was imagined to be a cutting instrument, with its heavy round end shaped for the hand and its pointed end giving the human body a new set of abilities to cut into the world.

These objects produced by what Prestwich evocatively called "blows applied by design" had been found in geological layers containing bones of animals thought to have lived in an epoch long before the human. A new alliance between geology and archaeology had literally repositioned human culture within geology itself – detailing the evidence of human inventiveness in the absence of any human remains in a kind of archaeology of the mind. Prestwich insisted that "the argument does not rest upon the evidence of skill, but upon the evidence of design."[2] The objects were not just made, they were thought. They were neither accidental effects of breaking stones nor copies of existing objects. Stones chipped by natural forces get ever more irregular whereas Prestwich observed that these "artificial" stones get more regular with each chip – "more and more finish, form, and evident art." They are human artifacts because the regularity of the shape "surely implies design, the application of forethought, and an intelligent purpose." The physical implement is first and foremost an instrument of thought.

The archaeologists stare obsessively at the object, measuring it, drawing it, and holding it in their own hands. They feel its weight and the transformation of their own body, imagining themselves as primitive, as if imagining the birth of humanity in the birth of technology. In their portrait of the human becoming human, found stones were used as hand tools to make a better hand tool. The evidence of forethought, of thinking ahead, is in the shape of this piece of stone, the sense of design — as if design is precisely that, a form of thinking ahead. Without even having to say it, the reading of the object depends on the idea that the human is a designer. Yet the only certain information the archaeologists had is a meticulous description of the physical object and the geological layer in which it was found, with detailed sectional drawings of the dig trying to locate the object in time by pinpointing the location of each find and the layering of all adjacent fossils, bones, tusks, teeth, shells, soil, rocks, gravel, minerals, and plants.

Evidence of such "designedly made" objects that had been "shaped by art and man's device," as Evans put it, shockingly overturned the self-image of humanity.[3] The religiously based agreement that the species was six

thousand years old was abruptly challenged by the idea of an extended human prehistory. The human was suddenly so much older than previously thought.

Just six months later, *Charles Darwin*← published *On the Origin of Species by Means of Natural Selection*. The transformative book embraced the idea that humans were ancient but more radically rejected the idea that any organism, including the human, had been designed by a divine intelligence. Darwin scandalously argued that the relentlessly impressive appearance of a "unity of design" throughout the organic world is actually a product of the essential mutability of all species. Countless incremental adaptions increase the chances of survival in changing environments. Clearly defined organisms with precise functions are paradoxically the product of extreme malleability. The *human eye→*, to use one of Darwin's examples, is the product of millions of minute variations in millions of minute elements over millions of years. It has an extremely long ongoing history, evolving from a simple nerve covered in pigment in primeval organisms into a highly sophisticated "living optical instrument" that is perfectly adjusted to human needs. The organ is so well adjusted to its task that is "scarcely possible" to avoid imagining that it has been designed analogously to the way humans design instruments — as when the analogous instrument of the telescope has been "perfected by the long-continued efforts of the highest human intellects."[4] Yet nothing in the organic world is the product of such a designing intellect. Natural selection is design without a designer.

For Darwin, the human ability to design does not set it apart from other animals. His follow-up book, *The Descent of Man in Relationship to Sex* started with the "indispensable" proof of the antiquity of humans demonstrated by the discovery of ancient designed stone tools.[5] The species in its current state is clearly "the most dominant animal that has ever appeared on the Earth." It is capable of astonishing levels of invention and control, independently inventing new tools everywhere on the planet since deepest antiquity. There is an immense difference between the human mind and that of an ape. Yet the difference is only one of degree.

Even if apes are unable to think of refashioning stones into a more precise tool, they do use stones as tools for fighting and opening nuts, make platforms for sleeping, and reason. Darwin insists that human intelligence does not necessarily progress. It can also regress and only differs by degree from that of other animals like the apes, which in turn only differ by degree from other species, even if that difference is again immense, and so on to include every organism on the planet. The human was not only a prehistoric creature living on Earth much earlier than previously imagined, as revealed by technological fossils, but it is embedded in a genetic continuum as a biological relative of all species that ultimately descend from a single original primeval life-form.

This double revolution dramatically transformed thinking about mentality, biology, and technology. The revolutions were interlinked, with human prehistory being a requirement of the idea of countless little biological variations over extremely long periods that allow for the appearance of design. Darwin financially supported some of the archaeological digs by the very people, like John Evans, who had first authenticated the ancient tools. He even speculated that starting to use stone tools would have affected the evolution of the shape of human hands by favoring the hands best suited to manipulating those tools – a speculation in a routinely overlooked passage that has only recently been confirmed.[6] The human hand is uniquely adapted to make and use tools.[7] The inherited structure of the body is ultimately altered by its technological extensions. For all Darwin's opposition to the idea of a designer of nature, the human can actually change the shape of its own organism over countless generations. Human designs eventually redesign the human. We are gradually redesigned by our tools.

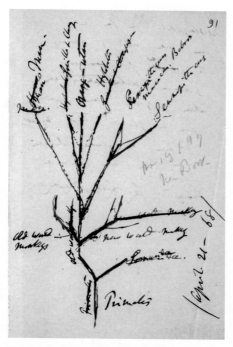

Darwin's family tree of the primates

This shocking encounter with prehistoric humanity and the blurring of any line between human and animal coincided with the equally shocking encounter with extreme industrialization in the mid-nineteenth century. The sustained attempt to develop and promote a concept of "design" in everyday objects as a necessary response to the massive impact of industrialization on human life was made during the dramatic encounter with the design of the very first tools and with a destabilizing sense of human intimacy with apes and the extended organic world. The emergent discourse about modern design became entangled with

this new sense of prehistory and primeval origins. The contemporary progress of design was overlapped onto a sense of deep time – as already became obvious when the very stone tools that had finally been authenticated in 1859 were placed at the center of the 1867 *Universal Exposition of Art and Industry in Paris*←. The innermost ring of the vast elliptical exhibition building devoted to all dimensions of human endeavor was a display of the "history of labor" in the gallery surrounding the central garden. The chronological display started with the earliest stone tools alongside the bones of extinct animals and then passed through ever more smooth and polished stone tools and on through five thousand objects of applied art from France in a series of rooms for each period from the Bronze Age up to the year 1800. This polemical promenade of design objects was interpreted as "an exposition of the mental development of the human race."[8] The massive global portrait of industry and culture from around the world at the exposition was literally wrapped around a didactic portrait of the evolution of design. Design itself was understood as the very principle of human evolution in an uncritical celebration of progress – as if nothing was more human than the ability to modernize oneself.

The concept of modern design that was already being incubated in these years didn't simply rest on the newly established concepts of human biological and technological evolution. Rather, it was part of the ongoing testing of those concepts. Both the biological and technological arguments had an extended history. The first publication of detailed drawings of stone "weapons" found alongside "extraordinary" bones of extinct animals had already been made in 1800 by John Frere, along with a speculation that they might come from "a very remote period indeed; even beyond that of the present world."[9] Mammoth bones were obsessively studied in the 1820s and started to be associated with finds of stone tools in many different countries in the 1830s but the overlap in time of human artifacts and animal fossils remained an implausible speculation. Jacques Boucher de Perthes transformed the argument by having a geologist prepare detailed drawings of the geological layers where he first started finding stone tools in 1841. He published his "geo-archaeology" claim that he had found many such "axes" (*haches*) in the same layers as extinct mammoths in his self-published 1847 book on primitive industry and the arts at their origin.[10] But the scientific community was not convinced. The turning point a decade later was the ability to use the relatively new technology of photography to take two images on April 27, 1859, of a stone tool sticking out from the side of an ancient layer 17 feet down one of de Perthes's digs near Saint-Acheul in the Lower Somme river valley in France. Prestwich and Evans were present as the embedded object was uncovered and *documented→*.[11] They were disappointed that it turned out to be a much more crudely formed object than most of the ones they had seen and drawn, an "unfinished implement," making the case for design more difficult. But the antiquity of such objects could now be demonstrated. They returned to England with the object the very next day, quickly confirmed similar evidence of prehistoric design in local digs and immediately reported to the scientific community, showing the object and the photograph – noting the similar findings that had been made France, England, Belgium, Germany, Italy, and Brazil. The sense of time was permanently revolutionized and the ever-expanding field of prehistory was unleashed as a form of permanent self-reflection on the species through a restless debate about the meaning of technofossils.

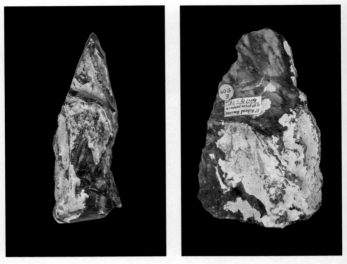

The unfinished stone tool presented to the Royal Society by Prestwich and Evans

Darwin's religiously unacceptable suggestion that humans might have descended from apes made shortly afterward was likewise built on a much longer tradition of thinking by a number of writers, including his own grandfather Erasmus Darwin, who speculated at the end of the eighteenth century about a continuous evolutionary development from microorganisms to contemporary society. Yet the idea of natural selection that Darwin had formulated and detailed by 1844 and finally published in 1859 was quickly surrounded by critiques and alternative theories. It would take a substantial amount of time to be generally accepted, and it still remains contentious – as does the status of prehistoric artifacts.

In fact, the purpose of the carefully shaped symmetrical hand axe that launched the whole debate was never clear and is still unclear today. The apparent presence of design was treated as the oldest evidence of the human, but design for what exactly? Prestwich already noted in his lecture to the Royal Society that most of the hundreds of ancient artifacts being lifted out of the ground looked like they had never been used: "as sharp and fresh-looking as though they had but recently come from the hands of the workman."[12] The sheer number of them had at first made Darwin doubt that they were human-made tools at all, and he sympathized with one of the responses to Prestwich's lecture that if they were human, then humans must have spent all their time chipping stones.[13] But he was soon persuaded by his closest colleagues and added a passage to 1861 American edition of *Origin of Species* that eagerly embraced the discovery of stone tools as definitive evidence that man "existed at a period very remote if measured in years."[14] He was fascinated with the subject yet still hesitated as to the meaning of human design. He saw the production of the first crafted tool as a very minimal functional improvement on found splinters of stone that could be used as tools and was particularly struck by the fact that it took "an immense interval of time" until Neolithic humans updated the technology with more refined and polished shapes.[15] Human tools are able to permanently reshape the human body but do not necessarily evolve under functional and environmental demands.

In the end, the design of the earliest tools might be as much about their ornamental beauty as about defined function, visually striking designs to help the survival of the craftsperson's genes by attracting mates. The crafted shape of a tool could be like the elaborate display of colored feathers of a peacock and all the other seemingly unnecessary structures, colors, and

HOXN
S.A.L.

First hand axe to
be published, 1800

patterns in the natural world. Darwin explained all this "ornament" with his crucial concept of "sexual selection" that supplemented "natural selection." He devoted a huge amount of his texts to the question of ornament as a major evolutionary force in the natural world, marveling at its diversity. More than half of *The Descent of Man* was about the question of ornament. It goes through the countless modes of "decoration" in animals before making a detailed account of all the ways that ancient and contemporary humans use an array of "artificial ornaments" and actively reshape every part of their bodies, often through dramatic painful physical modifications. The point is that these modes of self-fashioning actually bind humans closer to nature and the animal world rather than separates them from it. Even the uniquely naked skin of the human body is portrayed as the evolutionary consequence of an aesthetic choice. Given all the "strange" characteristics that are appreciated by different animals, Darwin finds it unsurprising that the loss of hair could be "esteemed as ornamental" by our "semi-human" ancestors, even as it created a real survival disadvantage in both hot and cold parts of the planet.[16]

This permanently complicates the archaeologist's foundational gesture of using design as evidence of human thought and life. The most carefully and repeatedly made tools are not necessarily made to be used. The exhibition of design itself may even be the primary goal of some of the oldest of human objects. It is as if they were made to look like they had been made. Their sharply defined form is an enigma – a puzzle at the intersection between human design and the design of the human. If design is the first sign of the human, it is the beginning of a permanent question.

Design has gone viral. The word *design* is everywhere. It pops up in every situation. It knows no limit. We are ambushed by wave upon wave of design biennials, weeks, fairs, festivals, neighborhoods, capitals, stores, magazines, books, websites, blogs, awards, programs, schools, centers, departments, museums, exhibitions, associations, councils, committees, and congresses. Along with "designer" hotels, drugs, bodies, and food we can have "happiness by design," "diplomacy by design," "social impact design," or "design for social justice." A new wave of "designers" shape "experience," "interfaces," "software," "brand," and "interaction." New university programs are devoted to "biological design" and "social innovation design." "Design thinking" has become a dominant business model affecting everything from politics to education, personal relationships, research, communication, and philanthropy. At a time in which the largest company in the world has based all its success on design, business schools now have design programs and the position of Chief Design Officer has recently assumed the same status as Chief Financial Officer. Companies that had nothing to do with design now build design into every dimension of corporate life. Politicians believe their success is dependent on design thinking. Cities have design departments whose role goes far beyond the usual focus on transportation, buildings, parks, street furniture, and signage to brand themselves. Even experts in "design risk assessment" have appeared to evaluate the danger that the incorporation of design brings to any scene. Design has become dangerously successful.

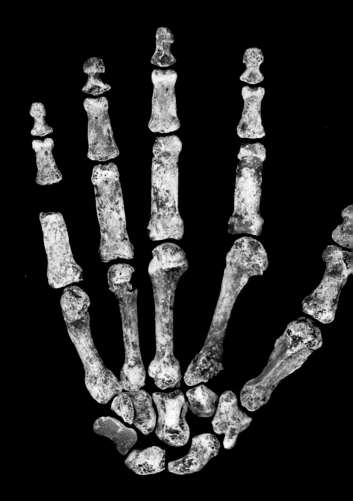

"The human hand is human because of what it makes, not of what it is."

—André Leroi-Gourhan

Homo naledi hands with features of both climbing trees and tool manipulation

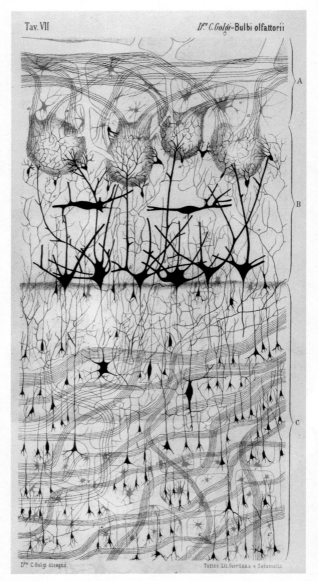

Camillo Golgi's technique to reveal paths of nerves in the brain, 1875

4

THE INVENTION
OF THE HUMAN

The question "Are we human?" immediately
triggers a chain of parallel questions: What
is human? When did we become human?
Are we still human? Were we ever human?
and Are we human yet?

The human might be the species that asks this kind of
question of itself, yet the very act of asking indicates that
there is no clear line between human and nonhuman.
Despite its massive impact on, under, and above the planet
and its apparent domination of other species, the human
is never unambiguously distinct from the animal or from
the wider systems of the Earth. Which raises an even more
fundamental question about this human animal: How
was the human invented? In other words, how did a self-
questioning species emerge? And what role did design play?

The emergence of the human through the continuous
invention of artifacts involves an uncanny mirroring. The
human becomes human in seeing itself in the things it
makes, or seeing its possibility in those things. So the
human doesn't simply invent tools. Tools invent the human.

More precisely, tool and human produce each other. The artifacts that prosthetically expand thought and reach are what make the human human. As Bernard Stiegler, reading the work of the influential paleoanthropologist André Leroi-Gourhan, puts it: "The prosthesis is not the mere extension of the human body; it is the constitution of this body qua 'human.'"[1] Leroi-Gourhan echoed the nineteenth-century idea that the human species was unique in evolving organically through its technological extensions: "The whole of our evolution has been oriented toward placing outside ourselves what in the rest of the animal world is achieved inside by species adaption."[2] The body itself is only human by virtue of technology: "the human hand is human because of what it makes, not of what it is."[3] What is human is the gesture of externalization, which is not from some preexisting interior, like thoughts in the brain, but is a gesture that constitutes a new sense of interior. The human is always being invented as such by the gestures that transform it. Brain, body, and artifact cannot be separated. Thinking only occurs in the intermingling between them. Artifacts themselves are thoughts that potentially also trigger new modes of thought.

The human brain is therefore an effect of new tools rather than the generator of new tools. Tools are an opportunity for it rather than an accomplishment of it. The intentionality and anticipation of effects that is distinctly human arises from the activity of making itself. Human intentions are provoked by making tools rather than executed by them.[4] And what makes a tool a tool? Strictly speaking, a tool is not produced to carry out a defined utilitarian task. Tools are born as challenges to existing concepts of utility. They open up new understandings of what could be useful. Utility is not a given unambiguous need. Ambiguity about utility is what drives new forms of utility.

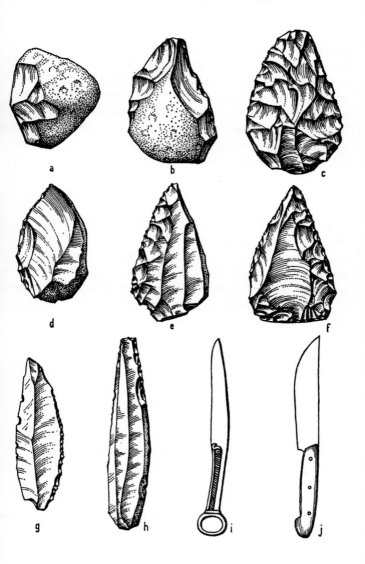

Leroi-Gourhan's illustration of evolution of the knife

Some paleoanthropologists argue that the main driver of human accomplishment is simply a uniquely human capacity for variability, an impulse to generate a multiplicity of ways to do things in reaction to different circumstances.[5] This variability itself can be understood as design capacity. When other species have figured out a way to do something, they keep repeating it forever until changes in the context reinforce a different direction. Humans continuously imagine different ways even in the same context, to the point of malfunction. The human is the only species that has tools that don't work, which is paradoxically the origin of its intelligence.

Design might simply be a name for this impulse to do things differently. Earlier attempts to explain the apparent exponential acceleration of human invention in the last 40,000 years presupposed some sudden increase in the cognitive capacity of the human brain as the enabling trigger. Recent accounts see this acceleration of invention occurring more gradually throughout the last 200,000 years, finding no evidence in fossils of change in the cognitive capacity to design. The ever-increasing size of groups in proximity to one another and the connectivity between these groups through migration formed a collective brain more likely to invent alternative ways to do things.[6] As more and more people shared knowledge and the accuracy of the knowledge being passed between groups and generations increased, the frequency of invention increased and continuously reinvented the brain in a kind of chain reaction of design.

The human brain itself is a malleable artifact whose circuits are continually rearranged through engagement with material culture. It is an unfinished project with a forever uncertain future and an equally uncertain beginning. The idea of a sudden flourishing of design gives way to the thought, as Patrick Roberts puts it, that "there is no single evolutionary event or moment where the brain becomes definitively 'human.'"

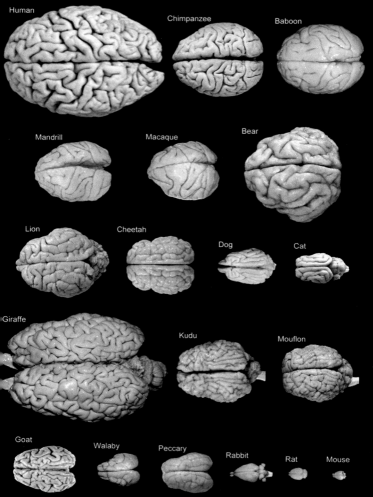

Human   Chimpanzee   Baboon

Mandrill   Macaque   Bear

Lion   Cheetah   Dog   Cat

Giraffe   Kudu   Mouflon

Goat   Walaby   Peccary   Rabbit   Rat   Mouse

5 cm

The archaeology of design is not about gradual shifts or revolutionary leaps. Design is by definition unevenly distributed in space and time, often flickering as some innovations disappear for a very long time only to be reinvented again. There is wide technological variability at any one time with the specific tools and ornamental sets reflecting behaviors in response to specific contexts. This variability itself ultimately contributes to the inventiveness of the species. The human invented by its artifacts is nowhere the same.

The incalculable diversity and interdependency of species on the planet that results from incremental adaptions to changing environments, including adaptions to the adaptions of others, finds its echo within the human species and is accelerated through the technological extensions that are an intimate part of its biology. Nothing could be more natural. The invention of artifacts that reinvent the inventor is precisely not controlled by the human in the sense of a singular animal imposing itself on the surrounding living world. The human is permanently suspended between

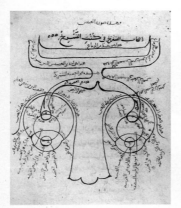

Ibn al-Haytham, ca. 1027

Khalifa ibn Abi al-Mahasin al-Halabi, 13th

being the cause and the effect, between designing living systems and being designed by them.

What is human in the end is neither the designer nor the artifacts but their interdependency. It is precisely the fully organic condition of technological life, the fact that it is alive, that raises the urgent questions about design. In particular, it raises the question of how, where, and when invention itself was invented. How did that impulse to do things differently arise?

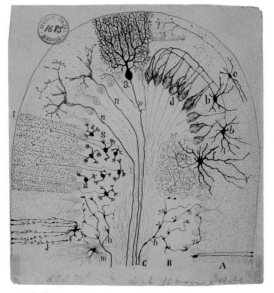

Cerebellum, Santiago Ramón y Cajal, 1904

Design is always understood to be a good thing. The empire of design reinforces the idea that good design is good business that makes good people. This concept has been so successfully promoted that all design is thought to be good design. The word *good* no longer even needs to be said. The very word *design* already means "good" – as if we don't need to think about the fact that the same concept is active in weapons, surveillance, invasions, policing, nationalism, incarceration, and terrorism. Good design might not be such a good thing.

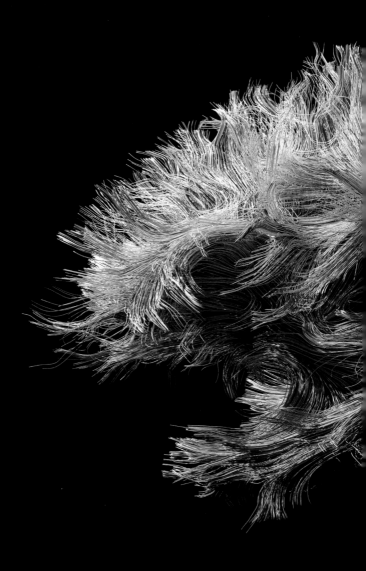

Diffusion MRI image of brain

"All that we do, almost all the time, is design, for design is basic to all human activity."

–Victor Papanek

35,400-year-old cave painting, Sulawesi Island, Indonesia

5

THE ORNAMENTAL SPECIES

Archaeologists and paleoanthropologists have long tried to understand why it took so long for the human to act like a human.

Until recently, there seemed to be a huge gap between the appearance of the anatomically modern *Homo sapiens* with its uniquely agile hands and large brain 200,000 years ago in Africa and the "behaviorally modern" human that appeared around 40,000 years ago. The symptoms of recognizably human behavior were the sophistication and complexity of tools, symbols, burial rituals, and techniques. Even then, this acceleration only became exponential in the last 12,000 years, when "humans redesigned themselves as organic beings," as John Hoffecker puts it, with abstract thinking, composite tools, long-distance networks of production and exchange, cooperative labor, and so on. Countless inventions steadily transformed the species and dramatically altered its relationship to the environment through the "domestication (that is, *re*designing) of plants and animals."[1]

From the deep time perspective of geology, the human ability to redesign itself and the living environment happened only yesterday. But the apparent gap between human anatomy and behavior has been rapidly dissolved by recent findings of ever-earlier evidence of distinctly modern human behavior in the fossil records. The fixation on the period from 40,000 years ago turns out to have been a Eurocentric bias concentrating on the time that *Homo sapiens* finally started arriving in Europe, having migrated out of Africa in waves starting as early as 135,000 years ago. The Eurocentrism of archaeology and anthropology has been undermined, for example, by the discovery in 2014 that some stenciled images of *human hands in a cave*↓ in Indonesia are at least 40,000 years old, preceding anything similar found in Europe, as do the oldest images of animals yet found, painted at least 35,400 years ago in the same cave.[2] The appearance of these key symptoms of modern behavior more or less simultaneously in the most dispersed places on the planet where the species had migrated undoes conventional wisdom. The human is not a European invention after all. Nor is it so young given the recent discoveries that elaborate burials, geometric engravings, and ornamental beads are already evident more than 100,000 years ago in Africa and the Middle East.

The finding of very old *ornamental beads↓* is crucial.
Ornaments are a key symptom of the human ability to
externalize its thoughts in symbolic form – generating
and sharing information rather than simply processing
it. Archaeologists treat marine shells with holes punched
in them to be strung together in necklaces as a pivotal
"information technology" that establishes a sense of self
and group identity. It is a "media of communication"
that broadcasts personal information to strangers who
are close enough to understand the meaning of your
ornaments but not close enough to already know you
personally. The ornaments simultaneously create a sense
of self and foster ever-wider social networks by aiming at
this middle distance between locals and strangers.[3] The
discovery of such shells in layers dated between 135,000
and 120,000 years old has completely overturned previous
accounts of the emergence of the human.[4] As the evidence
of communication through ornament gets ever older,
human inventiveness appears to get ever closer to the
anatomical beginning of the species.

Ornament both marks and expands the human. It is both
a sign of the ability to invent and the very mechanism

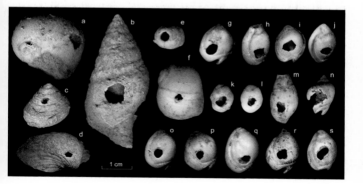

of invention. The systematic use of shells very far from their marine source is a symptom of crossing demographic thresholds and creating long-distance networks that further increases the odds of technological innovation. Symbolic behavior fosters the capacity for more complex tools, techniques, and strategies, rather than the other way around.

It is not ornament per se that defines the species. Neanderthals, the hominoid species genetically closest to *Homo sapiens* that became extinct 40,000 years ago, also used marine shells in parallel to modern humans. Ornament is essential to the life of animals in the most obvious sense of systematic visual patterns operating as an information system tied into survival through sexual reproduction. What is uniquely human is the chain reaction, the continuous reinvention of the human triggered by the invention of artifacts that create the conditions for further such inventions. This creative capacity to invent ultimately plays a survival function as utilitarian as that of any other tool but does so indirectly by constantly introducing potential new forms of utility. The immediate practical necessities to support life might not be sufficient. There is no survival advantage in having a tool that kills animals more efficiently if you cannot find sexual partners to reproduce. An attractive or intriguing artifact might ultimately be more practical than a seemingly practical one in offering the potential of other ways to do things. Ornament in this sense is both a tool of communication and the opening to new forms of tool – or at least there is finally no clear or permanent line between ornament and tool. The human cannot think of one without the other and precisely what is human is to think about this. Or, to say it another way round, the human is that species that keeps reflecting on the possible uses of its artifacts and communicating these reflections by making new artifacts, flickering back and forth between ornament and tool.

The invention of the human was never simply about the ability to make tools as such. *Stone tools*↓ as old as 3.3 million years have been found, long before the different hominin species. Even the hand axe associated with *Homo erectus*, with its consistent teardrop shape in comparison to the more random shapes of earlier tools, is as old as 1.7 million years. Its symmetry – which required a huge investment of energy and a series of different tools and striking techniques to produce – offered no apparent functional advantage over the previous tools and it is found in very large numbers with so many having no traces of ever being used. The status of these obsessively crafted objects was already a puzzle when they were found and discussed for the first time in the mid-nineteenth century. That puzzle has only deepened as the artifacts that preceded them have been found, favoring the possibility that the object was made to be looked at, tool as ornament, with its beauty offering a sexual advantage as a kind of advertisement of the good genes of whoever made it, as Darwin's theory allows.[5] Such a tool was already externalized thought, evidence of a proto-mind coinciding with a major increase in brain and body size.[6]

3.3-million-year-old tool found at Lomekwi, Kenya

1.4 million years old   300,000 years old

This is a collective mind as the artifact that is systematically shaped beyond its material function was continually remade, seen, and shared between groups and between generations, becoming incrementally more precise with minor local variations. Yet the same basic shape was produced in the same way without major adjustment for over a million and a half years across Africa, the Middle East, Asia, and Europe until the invention of a succession of ever more refined and complex tool sets marked the emergence of creativity itself and "the redesigned human."[7] Or, in Slavoj Zizek's words, "the very birth of humanity out of design."[8]

The use of a specific red-colored ochre for bodies and objects – carefully selected, ground into pigment, and transported over long distances – likewise precedes *Homo sapiens*. It has been found in layers as old as 500,000 years ago, even though the pigment is much less likely to have survived in the fossil records than stone. There is much debate about whether this use of pigment could have been symbolic, but there is general agreement that the addition of beads as body ornamentation is the crucial step associated with the emergence of human inventiveness that was associated with a massive growth in the use of red pigment.[9] The new use of beads as a form of information technology was itself remarkably stable, with evidence of the same shells being used across vast territories for tens of thousands of years with only minor shifts in the manufacture and design of these "thinking strings."[10] It was a default "design tradition" that likely acted as the most basic element of more complex design systems.[11] This new complexity of symbolic design precedes and becomes entangled with the new complexity of tools that combined many parts made of multiple materials able to be assembled in different ways that is evident around 65,000 years ago in the ever-changing fossil records and likely to be found ever earlier.

It is this multiplicity and malleability itself that is evidence of the capacity to invent that makes us human, that invents the human even. The ability to go beyond what is needed, to make something different or differently is crucial. The making of useless things, or things whose use has yet to be discovered, makes all the difference. Yet for that very reason, nothing in the fossil record, nor any artefact of contemporary life today, can simply be divided between useful and useless, tool and ornament. More often than not, what is seen as ornament is doing the real work and what looks like a tool is really for show. And the vibration between them is the very engine of design. Nothing is more serious than ornament if we really want to address the human ability to invent a planetary-sized ecology of technology as a designed form of organic life.

Design routinely constructs radical inequalities. The expansion of the capacity of one group is done at the expense of another group. At the same moment that every element of our world is being designed, that businesses and government deploy "design thinking," and the planet itself has become a human artifact, billions of people are on the edge of survival. It is not that there is a privileged world of design and an unprivileged world outside design. Design is not simply concentrated where wealth is concentrated. Rather it is everywhere, and it engineers concentrations of wealth and privilege. The spaces in which people and resources are exploited have been designed. They are the result of systematic decisions over centuries sustained by the latest technological and administrative systems. The apparent lack of design in vast parts of the world – the Arctic, the Amazon, the desert, the oceans, the atmosphere – is a mirage, a deadly effect. Inequalities are being crafted in everything we see, don't see, or don't want to see.

77,000-year-old incised ochre
Blombos Cave, South Africa

"Technology wasn't
invented by humans.
Rather the other way
around."

—Jean-François Lyotard

Are We Nothing But Machines II,
Mia-Jane Harris

6

NEWS FROM
NOWHERE

The thought of the posthuman is not what
happens after twentieth-century modern
design. On the contrary, modern design
was a reaction to that thought.

Just four years after Charles Darwin dramatically complicated thinking about the design of the human, the writer
Samuel Butler published his 1863 polemic "Darwin among
the Machines," the first of his speculations that the tools that
humans had originally deployed as prosthetic extensions
of their bodies were now evolving as living species in their
own right. Technology itself had become biological, a form
of "mechanical life" that was already deploying humans to
nourish it. It was just a matter of time before the machine
world would have no need of its human slaves to keep it
alive: "we are ourselves creating our own successors...these
glorious animals."[1] The possibilities that humans may either
become superhuman or have manufactured their own
demise were already a subject of public debate.

The image of the human as a prosthetic being that expands
its biology and mentality with layers of technology is both
the image of the prehistoric emergence of the species with
the first stone tools and the image of an inevitable future
where the fleshy body is left behind. In a sense, modern
design was incubated with an eye to these two new

horizons, as if suspended between them. With the dramatic acceleration of industrialization in the mid-nineteenth century, workers were increasingly treated as disposable machine parts and machines were treated as organisms with an internal life that needed to be preserved. This reversal became the focus of much public discussion, with many writers speculating on the possible demise of the human at the hands of the mechanized world that it had produced. In an international debate lasting more than half a century, modern design was itself designed as an instrument to engage with the biology of the machine world in a way that supposedly both affirms and protects the human.

The construction of the basic argument for what would eventually be labelled "good design" involved hundreds of voices. A whole series of new institutions were set up in different countries — including associations, schools, museums, and magazines. Countless political, financial, regional, national, local, personal, and professional agendas were involved. It was a massive, extended, uneven, and nuanced debate. Yet the core of the argument remained surprisingly consistent. Design was framed as a way to deal with the increasingly dominant logic of the industrialized and globalized world while resisting the perceived dehumanizing impact of that world.

Each designer and design theorist in the ongoing discourse was obliged to take a position on the relationship between human and machine. It was not so much a discussion about particular forms as it was about the possible relationship of these forms to the human and technological worlds. The debate flickered back and forth between the sense that technology is the greatest threat to our humanity and the sense that technology might be the most human thing about us, since only the human invents tools to make tools and has always used its own artifacts to reinvent itself. In a sense, the debate about design was looking for a way to preserve both thoughts, constructing design as a way to both reinvent and protect the human.

The concept of modern design that is now a routine part of most dimensions of everyday life was originally a reaction to the exponential acceleration of mechanization in the so-called Industrial Revolution that was initiated in England and expanded itself across the planet as a vast interconnected mechanism digesting ever more territory, resources, and people. The rapid massive shift from the energy of humans and horses to that of machines, compounded by the revolution of time and space with the emergence of train networks, and compounded again with the arrival of instantaneous communication by telephone, telegraph, and radio was itself seen as an all-consuming life-form with its own biological needs and even desires. The acceleration of industrialization was accompanied by an increasingly urgent questioning of what constitutes the human. The word *design* was called on in the 1830s to explicitly negotiate between human and machine in a discourse that again started in England, migrated to continental Europe, and kept expanding to eventually become global in a kind of belated echo of industrialization itself. The concept of design (and even the use of the word *design*) that was developed by this debate and is itself now a global commodity, remains a nineteenth-century product.

The British government was convinced in the 1830s that Prussia and France would dominate the newly emerging global market because their industrial arts were of a higher quality. They tried to emulate the continental rivals by setting up a comprehensive infrastructure of schools, journals, museums, and programs of public education through lectures, exhibitions, and night classes.[2] The expression "School of Design" was invented in response to the wide array of institutions in Europe ranging from technical training centers to elite art academies, of which only the Royal Free School, founded in 1767 in Paris, included the word *dessin* (drawing) in its long title. For the British reformers, design was much more than drawing, even if training in drawing was fundamental. Rather, it was a morally infused way of making decisions about objects that galvanized government, business, industry, class, and art interests.

The basic idea was to spread knowledge of the "principles of design" to both the manufacturers of objects and the people who used them. These principles were simply the attempt to make ornament subservient to the form of the manufactured object and the form subservient to its function, underpinned by the quasi-aristocratic sense of "good taste." "Good" was the key word, linking a sense of morality to a sense of controlled aesthetics. "Good art" in everyday objects has "moral benefits."[3] It was thought that the exhibition of good design would raise the moral status of the designer in society. The design reformers occasionally suggested that their main commitment to "progress in good design" did not even require them to discuss morality itself.[4] The whole point is that the virtue of design is meant to be self-evident. Design itself was understood as a form of education. But the reformers never felt that they had made any progress in their campaign. After each major international exhibition, starting with the *Great Exhibition in the Crystal Palace of 1851→* that they had organized, the sense of local design inferiority deepened. Yet the feeling of failure acted as a kind of motivating engine and by the end of the century Germany and France were as jealous of British design culture as the British had originally been of them. Key writers like Adolf Loos and Hermann Muthesius used English design as their model and

Das Andere (The Other), edited by
Adolf Loos

the arguments that had been formed in England in the face of industrialization were imported when the epicenter of the debate moved to Germany. Muthesius, for example, had lived in England as a kind of cultural spy for the government and played an important role in setting up the Deutscher Werkbund in 1907 as a collaboration between designers, industry, and government to explicitly pick up the English arguments. Loos immediately attacked the Werkbund for its attempt to invent the design of the everyday object – preferring the ready-made simplicity of English objects. Yet the Werkbund's eventual celebration of "form without ornament" would retroactively appear as a Loosian manifesto.

The different positions remained entangled with each other as the debate migrated. The work of those trying to defend the human from the machine often influenced those trying to embrace the machine and vice versa. This had already been the

case in England when the task of finding a philosophy of design appropriate for a machine age became energized by those most critical of the machine. *William Morris←*, for example, had led the view of the machine as a human tool that had now become a new life-form that was turning humans into its tools, as he argued in his 1886 lecture:

I am thinking of the modern machine, which is as it were alive, and to which the man is auxiliary, and not of the old machine, the improved tool, which is auxiliary to the man, and only works as long as his hand is thinking.[5]

Morris appealed to preindustrial craft and polemically withdrew from the enslaving space of the factory to his own workshops, yet he played an active role in the ongoing government attempt to develop a design culture in the schools of design, museums, and manufacturing. He submitted his own designs for machine-printed fabrics and carpets while warning against machines. At a government commission formed in 1882 to address the deficiencies of British design, he made it clear that he was not against the machine as such but against the enslavement of humans to machines. He advised the government that understanding the machine and industrialized manufacturing processes is "the very foundation of design."[6] In fact, Morris thought that the machines that had so damaged humanity by turning workers into machine parts were much better designed than the products made with them. His portrait of a socialist utopia resisting "mechanical life" in favor of human life in his novel *News from Nowhere* of 1890 includes "immensely improved machinery" capable of freeing workers to work on what they wanted to work on.[7]

The thinking of Morris actually became a model for many of those in the Werkbund debates that were trying to embrace the repetitive standardizing logic of the machine while reaffirming deeper human values that would supposedly control the machine. In a 1902 book that begins with an epigraph by Morris, Muthesius himself portrayed the machine as a thoroughly human artifact that simply needs to be tamed by human will: "the machine itself, however, is simply an improved tool. To exclude it as such from our human production would be foolish."[8] The back and forth in the continuous dialogue that incubated modern design was never really a back and forth between the separate needs of the machine and the needs of the human. Rather it was an engagement with the complexity of the disquieting interdependency of human and machine. The participants in the famous Werkbund debate about the merits of standardization at Cologne in 1914, for example, exaggerated their differences. Most of those who responded to Muthesius's call for the standardization of design with a counterdemand for the preservation of individual expression quietly changed sides immediately after the polemical confrontation. Some, like Walter Gropius, would even become the very spokespeople of the necessity for machine age standardization. The main currency on both sides was always the "human," and the ultimate embrace of the machine was never in doubt.

The discourse shaping modern design remained full of these permanent paradoxes. The Berlin critic Adolf Behne cannily argued in 1926 that those designers who only care about the mechanical logic of function, and aim to make a building a "pure tool," actually end up with an anthropomorphic architecture: "In fact dehumanization is the very thing that leads to humanization, to anthropomorphism."[9] And in reverse, those who claim to care only about "human will" end up producing an inhumanly standardized architecture.

Behne insisted that from the first very first tools and shelters, architecture has always been a combination of function and play: "Primitive man is not simply utilitarian. He demonstrates his instinct for play even in his tools, which he makes smooth and beautiful beyond the demands of necessity, painting them or decorating them with ornaments."[10] There is no line between tool and toy. In fact, Behne argued that it is play that generates form in the first place. Function itself is unable to "arouse human interest in any way." Any attempt to separate function and play is foolish. The supposedly pure functionalist is actually more interested in redesigning humans than in function itself:

> The functionalist ... does not see [purpose]
> as something complete, unalterable, rigidly
> prescribed; rather, it is a means to broaden and
> refine, intensify and sublimate, move and mold
> human beings. For him every satisfied purpose
> is an implement for creating new, more refined
> human beings.[11]

Modern design keeps declaring its loyalty to the human but actually flips back and forth between ignoring the human and inventing a new one.

These paradoxes that were already triggered by the question "are we human?" in the mid-nineteenth century made their way from England into the Werkbund and then into the Bauhaus, across to the United States and then dispersed globally, and became embedded in the idea of good design that became the slogan for modern design after World War II. The promise of good design is to produce good humans. But this promise is inseparable from a globalized industrial complex that threatens humanity. Good design tries to hold back the disturbing thoughts that were so palpable in the nineteenth century that we might no longer be human or are obsolete in our very humanness. Good design tries to block the very thoughts that inspired the idea of modern design in the first place.

Design is also the design of neglect. In June 2015 eight-year-old Adou Ouattara, from Ivory Coast, was discovered by border control X-ray machines as he was being smuggled into Spain from Morocco inside a roller suitcase. Everyone could see into the small suitcase as the image went viral in all media. Likewise, we look down on an overcrowded boat off the coast of Libya in a drone photograph and they look directly back at us. In the pages of a Sunday magazine, we watch a ten-year-old boy named Hassan trying on a life vest in a shop in Izmir full of designer jeans in different styles and T-shirts piled up on the shelves and emergency clothing on the table. With the attentive shop assistant fitting the boy and the adult smiling in the mirror (presumably the father), the scene appears normal. Perhaps they are going on a boat trip. Emergency, and the role of design within it, has become routine as we all watch it. On August 5, 2010, a chunk of ice four times the size of Manhattan broke away from the ice shelf on the northwest coast of Greenland. Millions of people watched the video from a remote camera that had been set on the ice shelf just a few days before. The situation of the refugees and of climate change has been obvious for a very long time and is watched in real time by all, yet there is little action. The world has developed an ability to watch everything yet do nothing. This lack of action is also designed. Neglect has been shaped.

"These forms were born as though by magic! The spontaneous objectification of an idea springing from the dark, but wonderfully persistent, consciousness of the cave dweller."

–Henry van de Velde

Huge ice island breaks off northwestern
coast of Greenland, August 5, 2010

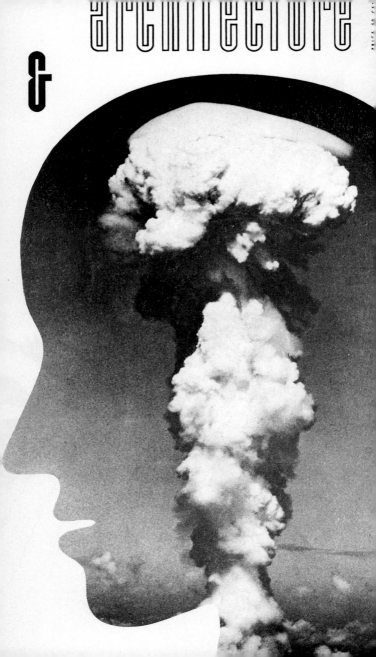

7

GOOD DESIGN
IS AN
ANESTHETIC

Good design is an anesthetic. The smooth
surfaces of modern design eliminate friction,
removing bodily and psychological sensation.

Good design is meant to be contagiously virtuous. Even
the smallest object, a door handle for example, is thought
to change the well-being, emotions, and thoughts of
whoever uses it, touches it, looks at it, or even reads about
it, and also the lives of whoever encounters those who have
encountered it, and so on in a kind of viral chain reaction
that ultimately transforms society.

A well-designed object is one that does ever more good
to ever more people. An ambition to social reform is
embedded in each seemingly modest project. Nineteenth-
century arguments about the morality of design still infuse
contemporary design discourse today – along with all
the complications, contradictions, and barely suppressed
violence that comes with any such declarations of a moral
high ground.

Good design is "an ethic rather than an aesthetic," as the
British architects Alison and Peter Smithson put it in the
1950s. Its goodness supposedly comes from the rejection

of any waste and the direct presentation of the facts –
finding whatever form and materials most efficiently resolve
all the practical demands of production and function.
Good design should be a surprise. It invents a novel way
to reduce any excess in the making, distributing, and using
of things. It gets rid of any external dissimulating layers
to uncover the hidden material facts, the material realities
that can be reorganized to liberate new social realities. No
outcome is prescribed. Yet good design has a recognizable
aesthetic. Good design looks like good design. It is
irreducibly associated with a certain visual smoothness. The
goal of reducing functional, economic, and social friction is
indistinguishable from a frictionless aesthetic that acts as a
kind of self-advertisement of design. So strong is this visual
effect, so reassuring and dazzling are the surfaces, that
it becomes unclear whether good design is doing good
things at all. The ethic turns out to be an aesthetic.

Modern design was launched in defense of smooth
surfaces. English Arts and Crafts design was on a path
toward simplification and seamless surfaces. The word
smooth played a big role. Already in 1894, Alfred Lichtwark,
the influential social commentator, museum director, and
pioneer of public art education programs in Germany,
praised the English model of "smooth walls" and "smooth,
polished, light forms" for furniture as having a "calming
effect" after the assaults of ornament.[1] Adolf Loos in
Vienna celebrated the surfaces made by metalworkers for
being "smooth and polished, no ornament, no decoration"
in a 1898 newspaper article.[2] Hermann Muthesius used
the English model in his much-discussed essay on "New
Ornament and New Art" (1901) where he called for a
"cleansing" away of ornament in favor of forms closer to
those of sailboats, electric lamps, and bicycles. Modern art
would be modern by virtue of its rejection of superfluous

ornament. The moral and physical health needs of "modern humanity" called for light and air and "smooth and simple furnishings" that are easy to clean – a "sanitation" of body and mind.[3]

Loos's famous essay "Ornament and Crime" (1908) inevitably celebrated what it called the "smooth object." It pointed to the "completely smooth" surfaces of shoes, cigarette cases, and gingerbread that are untainted by the "pathological" use of ornament that has "no human connections at all" for "modern man."[4] Cleansing anything superfluous was a moral project. Le Corbusier followed the argument closely, declaring in *Toward an Architecture* (1923), his most influential book, that "façades were smooth" in all the great periods.[5] People should be proud to live in the most modern of houses with walls as "smooth as sheet-iron," like the ancient walls of the perfected machine that is the Parthenon, where "the impression is of naked polished steel." Such smooth surfaces are "naked," "bare," "clear," "honest," "direct," "pure," "clean," "healthy," "moral" – a chain of synonyms used to create an atmosphere of polemical virtue. Aesthetics became ethics. Design in the machine age would necessarily be as smooth as the surfaces of the well-oiled machines that are allergic to friction. To embrace mechanization was to embrace "smooth…surfaces that are faultless."[6] Ornament is friction. It has to be flattened out into a plane.

One by one, modern designers identified their modernity by embracing "smooth surfaces butting up against other smooth surfaces," as Robert Mallet-Stevens put in 1924.[7] The cult of the smooth underpinned the extraordinary influence of the Bauhaus school directed by Walter Gropius in the 1920s. Despite a huge diversity of avant-garde experiments within his "factory," a singular recognizable industrial design aesthetic emerged that still represents the very idea of good design today. The inner needs of function turned out to be a visual effect, the effect of truth-telling, as if a smooth surface, a rounded corner, or a continuously folded metal tube could only tell the truth and that truth itself was beautiful.

This logic was reinforced in countless exhibitions and publications that were themselves treated as equally smooth interfaces with perfected layouts, posters, labels, and typefaces. The promotion of modern design was itself designed. There was even a genre of well-designed publications of well-designed exhibitions of well-designed objects. The public, patrons, professionals, manufacturers, officials, and critics were relentlessly trained to appreciate the virtue of modern design and given a language with which to describe it.

Since 1938 the Museum of Modern Art held travelling exhibitions of modestly priced "useful objects" for the household demonstrating the "aesthetic" virtue of "good modern design" in a machine age.[8] The museum acted as the arbiter of good taste, abandoning any line between museum and market. A Department of Industrial Design was created in 1939 and its first director, Eliot Noyes, a former student and employee of Walter Gropius, added a special section on "Good Design" in 1941 to the fourth edition of the popular *Useful Objects* series. A placard listed four principles of good design as "criteria which the spectator himself may apply in judging the design of other objects . . . thereby creating a demand which will tend to increase the number and general availability of well-designed objects."[9] The public was trained to recognize the aesthetics of modern design in the "contemporary sense of beauty" that combines function, material, and production

– the "graceful...handsome...simplicity...functional design," as the press release put it. The approach was echoed by Max Bill, a former student of the Bauhaus, in his 1949 *Die Gute Form* traveling exhibition of everyday objects for the Swiss Werkbund. In 1950 Edgar Kauffmann Jr. started the major series of *Good Design* exhibitions at MoMA with Charles and Ray Eames designing the first exhibition, and *Good Design labels*↑ were attached to the products being endorsed. This was imitated by endless international good design awards, exhibitions, and publications that continue the visual training program today. For all the supposedly self-explanatory goodness of its smooth surfaces, good design never speaks for itself. It is always labeled and surrounded by an army of earnest promoters describing its fusion of aesthetic and ethical virtue.

Design is never shocking, disturbing, alienating, incomprehensible, or discomforting in this global campaign. On the contrary, it is the antidote – offering identity, stability, efficiency, clarity, comfort, support, integration, and so on. Good design is resolved, responsive, healthy, and efficient. All good, all the time. Yet the very insistence on the morality of the smooth surfaces of modern design hints that things are not so simple. What is the human that needs this smoothness so badly? Or is made to feel needy, inadequate, wounded, or incomplete in the face of good design and offered the chance to rebuild itself by simply choosing the right product?

If Alfred Lichtwark had already welcomed the sedative
effect of smooth surfaces at the end of the nineteenth
century, Le Corbusier saw them as an anesthetic to calm
"the nerves shattered in the aftermath of war" at the
same time that actual anesthetics (cocaine) were being
"peddled" in the street of Paris.[10] *Cocaine* ← was one of the
first substances used as anesthetic for surgery by Karl Koller
(on the recommendation of Freud) in 1884. The history
of modern anesthetics uncannily parallels that of modern
design. *The first public demonstration* ↑ of an operation under
anesthesia (with ether) took place at Massachusetts
General Hospital in 1846.

Anesthesia is the removal of feeling, the temporal
suppression of the central nervous system in order to
achieve lack of sensation. *Aesthetics*, from the Greek, had
everything to do with sensation, with perception by bodily
feeling, and nothing to do with the intellect or the ideal
until the nineteenth century. The modern idea of aesthetics
as a branch of philosophy is contemporary with the age of
industrialization. Aesthetics in the modern sense is itself
therefore already an anesthetic – it has removed all bodily

sensation, all feeling. For Le Corbusier, even the touch of the modern object becomes a reassuring visual effect: "Our hand reaches out to it [the modern object] and our sense of touch *looks* in its own way as our fingers close around it."[11] Smooth white surfaces restore the "calm" that preceded the brutality of the arrival of all the mass-produced ornaments of modern industry. Le Corbusier repeatedly uses the word *calm* to represent the new beauty of the machine, the effect of putting all extra domestic objects into built-in storage, the demeanor of the modern engineer, and the final effect of mastering the world of mechanization that had so challenged humanity.

The shock of war, the shock of the machine, the shock of the metropolis have in common anesthesia, the temporary removal of feeling, whether physical or psychological. In "Experience and Poverty" (1933) Walter Benjamin wrote about people returning from World War I poorer in experience, unable to communicate, silent, in shock after feeling the full force of modern technology: "A generation that had gone to school in horse-drawn streetcars now stood in the open air, amid a landscape in which nothing was the same except the clouds, and, at its center, in a force field of destructive torrents and explosions, the tiny, fragile human body."[12] Feeling was no longer possible. Humans were anesthetized. This poverty of experience finds its parallel in modern architecture, in glass-and-steel buildings on whose smooth surfaces the inhabitant cannot leave any traces, any memory. In his writings on Baudelaire, Benjamin speaks of the smile of passersby in the metropolis ("keep smiling") that protect them from an unprecedented number of close encounters with strangers by developing mimetic tactics. The smile "functions as mimetic shock absorber."[13] Modern design is likewise a shock absorber, its frozen smile barely hiding the terror it tries to cover over.

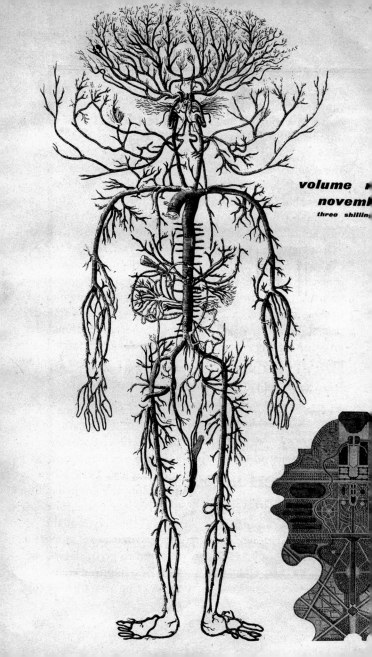

volume
novem
three shilling

Benjamin's understanding of modern experience is neuro-logical.[14] "The shock experience which the passer-by has in the crowd corresponds to what the worker 'experiences' at his machine."[15] War, machine, and metropolis are all shock environments, conditions of danger where one has to be able to react quickly to protect oneself from sudden, unforeseeable threats. Nerves are on the periphery.

The elimination of ornament is not simply an aesthetic choice but a neurological or even narcotic one. Loos argues that we no longer have the nerves to eat, dress, and decorate as in previous centuries. Modern man has a whole new set of nerves with completely different sensitivities. In "Ornament and Crime," he speaks of his "horror" in front of the decorated animals in culinary displays, particularly if he thinks he has to eat "one of these stuffed animal corpses. I only eat roast beef!" He feels the same nausea in the face of any excessive ornament, whether on food or architecture: "We lack the steady nerves to drink from an elephant's ivory tusk on which an Amazon battle scene has been engraved.... Our temples are no longer painted blue, red, green, and white, like the Parthenon, no, we have learned to appreciate the beauty of naked stone."[16]

A LA SORBONNE
Amphithéâtre Michelet
46, rue Saint-Jacques à 8 h. 45
Quatre conférences
en langue Allemande
ADOLF LOOS
"Der Mensch mit den modernen Nerven"
Vom Gehen, Stehen, Sitzen, Liegen,
Schlafen, Wohnen, Essen und
Sich-Kleiden
1926
Mercredi, le 17 Février   Jeudi, le 25 Février
Lundi, le 22 Février   Lundi, le 8 Mars
ENTRÉE LIBRE

The rejection of ornament is a physiological reaction, as Loos put it in 1919, when discussing the English military uniform as a model for modern dress: "The nerves of the modern man rebel against a demand to go back twenty, fifty, or a hundred years."[17] By 1921 he was arguing that the whole biology of man had evolved to *give modern man a whole new set of nerves*↙.[18] And in "Ornament and Education" (1924) he wrote: "Modern Man, the man endowed with a modern nervous system, doesn't need ornament. On the contrary, he loathes it. Every object that we call modern lacks ornament. Our dresses, our machines, our furs, and every object of everyday use don't have – since the French Revolution – any ornament."[19]

In "Karl Kraus," Walter Benjamin quotes Robert Scheu, brother of Gustav Scheu (for whom Adolf Loos built a controversial house in Vienna in 1912): "Kraus," writes Robert Scheu, "discovered a great subject that had never before set in motion the pen of a journalist: the rights of the nerves. . . . He became the advocate of the nerves . . . but the subject grew under his hands, to become the problem of private life."[20]

Private life, the interior, becomes newly fragile, like that of the nervous individual analyzed by psychoanalysis or the vulnerable body of the tuberculosis patient penetrated by X-rays. Everybody becomes like a child or a patient needing to be wrapped in soft lining. It is as if the new nerves are so new that the modern individual has only just been born and needs a protective incubator to survive, to gain the necessary strength. Loos's architecture is such an incubator.

Loos was himself fragile. He suffered from numerous nervous and physical ailments throughout his life and at the end, he checked himself into the sanatorium run by his friend the psychiatrist Dr. Schwarzmann, in Kalksburg, where he died in 1933. A year earlier, Buckminster Fuller had included "nerve shock proofing" in his list of basic requirements for all houses.[21] Frederick Kiesler and Richard Neutra would develop entire theories of design based on

the nerves. It is as if nerves themselves were the true clients
of modern design.

After World War II, Charles and Ray Eames defined design
itself as a "shock absorber." Involved during the war in the
military production of *leg splints* ↑ and body shells for injured
soldiers – shock absorbers for a traumatized body – they
developed these splints upon hearing that the metal Thomas
metal splint used by the army was causing further injury
because of amplified vibration during transport. If the
soft plywood splint holds the wounded leg so much more
tenderly than the Thomas splint, which led to gangrene
and death, the postwar house is for the Eameses no longer
just glass and steel where you cannot leave any traces,
as in the post–World War I house. The steel and glass is
just the frame to accommodate a galaxy of objects that
define a new lifestyle: "The house must make no insistent
demands for itself, but rather aid as a background for life
in work . . . and as re-orientator and 'shock absorber.'"[22]
The interior becomes a showroom full of objects. Shock is
absorbed through the consumption of design.

But what is this shock? Domestic life could no longer be taken for granted post–World War II. It became an art form carefully constructed and marketed by a whole new industry: a form of art therapy for a traumatized nation, a reassuring image of the "good life" to be bought like any other product. Instead of offering a complete environment to the postwar consumer, the Eameses offered a variety of components that individuals could construct and rearrange themselves. The shock in the postwar years is the shock of nuclear annihilation. "Good design" offers "good life," a galaxy of happy, self-contained objects for people who do not feel safely contained and cannot be sure of life itself. The Eameses perfected the "keep smiling" strategy. Perhaps no other designers can be seen smiling so often and so polemically. If the ever-scowling Adolf Loos had insisted in "Ornament and Crime" that the craftsman is "so healthy he cannot invent ornament," the ever-beaming Eameses, the poster children of good design, encourage the postwar consumer to keep clinging to smooth design as if to a psychological life raft. The real function of good design remains anesthetic, a symptom of a trauma that cannot be expressed, a smooth line of defense.

Today the mantra *human-centered design* is chanted again as the way to approach any question, as if the human is a specific knowable entity. It presupposes a kind of transparent human, which is such a fragile, utopian, or even dystopian idea. Freud insisted that real needs are the ones that can never be expressed: "The mind is like an iceberg, it floats with one-seventh of its bulk above water." The distinction between needs and desires is anyway never clear, and both are multiple and typically contradictory.

No one is even really sure about what they see looking back at them in the mirror in the morning in that poignant moment just before assembling some kind of self-design with which to navigate the outside world. The precise context of design is the indeterminacy of the human. Design has never been about giving someone or some group what they ask for but what they wish they had asked for and retrospectively pretend that they did ask for.

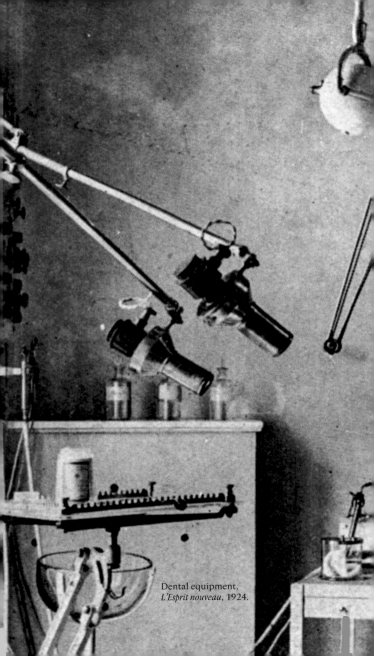

Dental equipment,
L'Esprit nouveau, 1924.

"From the start the greatest planetary terraformers (and reformers) of all have been and still are bacteria and their kin … No species, not even our own arrogant one pretending to be good individuals in so-called modern Western scripts, acts alone; assemblages of organic species and of abiotic actors make history, the evolutionary kind and the other kinds too."

–Donna Haraway

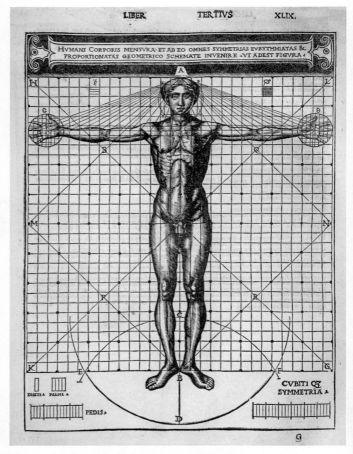

Measure of the human body, Cesariano's translation of Vitruvius, 1521

8

THE DESIGN
OF HEALTH

**Design is medicine. If classical theories of
the Greek polis followed theories of the
four humors, contemporary ideas of health
organize design theories today.**

Vitruvius in the first century BC launched Western architectural theory by insisting that all architects needed to study
medicine: "Healthfulness being their chief object."[1] He devoted a large part of the first of his *Ten Books on Architecture*
to the question of health. He gives detailed instructions
on how to determine the healthiness of a proposed site
for a city by returning to the ancient method of sacrificing
an animal that lives there and inspecting its liver to make
sure it is "sound and firm." Likewise for the healthy site of
each building, he discusses the theory of the four humors
at length and emphasizes the direction of the winds and
the sun. Too much of one humor enfeebles and "impairs
the fluids of the human body." In reverse, those who are
unwell can be cured more quickly through design, building
up the system of those "exhausted by disease," including
consumption. Vitruvius discusses the internal workings of
the body just as much as he discusses the internal working
of buildings. Established theories of medicine are used as
a kind of foundation for architectural theory. Architecture
itself becomes a branch of medicine.

As Renaissance schools of medicine used casts of body parts, design schools such as the Accademia del Disegno in Florence in 1563, used cast fragments of historical buildings for teaching, and anatomical dissection was a central part of the training. As doctors investigated the mysterious interior of the body by cutting into and dissecting it, architects tried to understand the interior of buildings by slicing section cuts through them. In the sketchbooks of Leonardo da Vinci, cutaway views of architectural interiors appear beside anatomical drawings. He understood the interiors of the brain and the womb in architectural terms, as enclosures that must be cut through to reveal their secrets. The central reference for architecture was no longer a whole body but a dissected, fragmented, analyzed body. Likewise in the mid-nineteenth century, Viollet-le-Duc illustrated his *Dictionnaire raisonné de l'architecture française du XI au XVIe siècle* (1854–68) with perspectival *exploded cuts*↘ showing medieval buildings as if dissected. Influenced by George Cuvier's *Leçons d'anatomie*

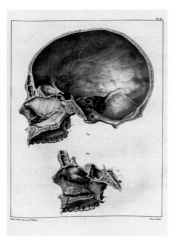

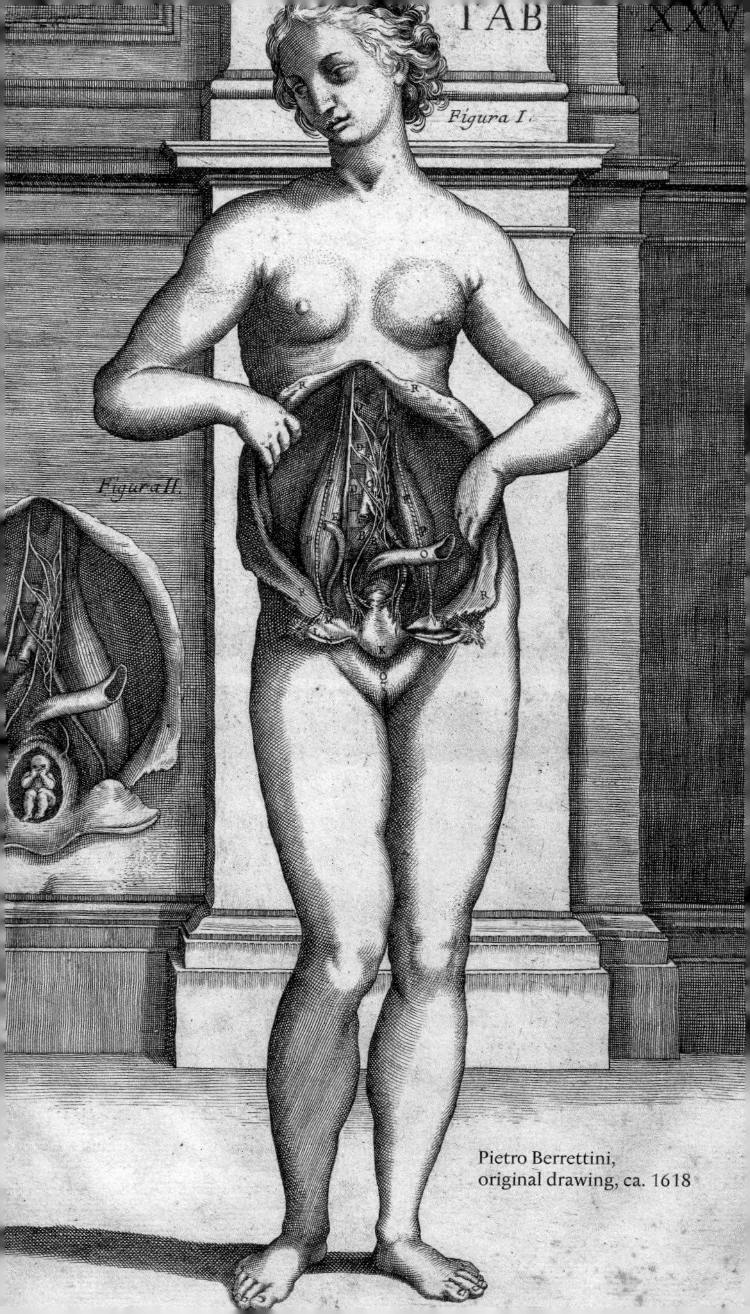

TAB XXV

Figura I.

FiguraII.

Pietro Berrettini,
original drawing, ca. 1618

comparée (1800–1805) and Jean-Marc Bourgery's *Traité complet de l'anatomie de l'homme, comprenant la médecine opératoire*, he treated medieval architecture as a body to be analyzed.

As medical representations changed, so did architectural representations. In the twentieth century, the widespread use of *X-rays→* made a new way of thinking about architecture possible. Modern buildings even started to

look like medical images, with transparent glass walls revealing the inner *secrets of the building←*. Indeed, the architecture of the early twentieth century cannot be understood outside of tuberculosis. The symptoms, if not the principles, of modern architecture seem to have been taken straight out of a medical text on the disease. A year before the German microbiologist Robert Koch discovered the tubercle bacillus in 1882, a standard medical

book gave as the cause of the disease, among other things, lack of exercise, sedentary indoor life, defective ventilation, deficiency of light, and depressing emotions.[2] It took a long time for these notions to lose credibility. Tuberculosis was thought to be a wet disease produced by damp cities. In an uncanny echo of Vitruvius, the TB patient was thought to need a new environment to dry out the inside of their bodies.

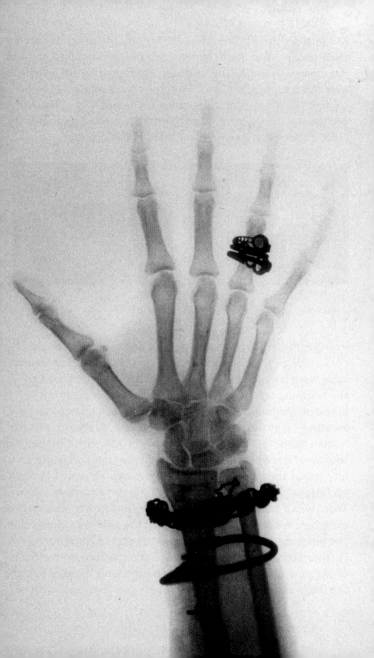

Modern architects offered health by providing exactly such a change of environment. Nineteenth-century architecture was demonized as unhealthy, and sun, light, ventilation, exercise, roof terraces, hygiene, and whiteness were offered as means to prevent, if not cure, tuberculosis. The publicity campaign of modern architecture was organized around contemporary beliefs about tuberculosis and fears of the disease.

"Historic Paris, Tubercular Paris,"
Le Corbusier, *La ville radieuse*, 1933

Alvar Aalto, Paimio Sanatorium,
Paimio, Finland, 1932

In engaging TB, architects were not just tuning in to one illness among others. As Susan Sontag has argued, few diseases have been so "spectacularly, and similarly, encumbered by the trappings of metaphor" as tuberculosis and cancer.[3] In his book *The Human Motor*, Anson Rabinbach goes as far as locating TB as part of a complete reconceptualization of the human body.[4] He argues that the obsession with fatigue that took over between 1895 and World War I marked rising anxiety about the industrial age. Diseases like TB were blamed on fatigue, and exercise programs offered to combat them. There was a widespread call for organized sports. Gymnastic exercises, which had been limited to the military throughout the nineteenth century, were now advocated for schools. Furthermore, the military itself was reorganized on the basis of the new "sciences of work." Medicine and biology became the basis of political theory. Through this "biologization of politics," the sciences of the body were firmly established as the basis of "social hygiene." By 1910 they were split into physiology and psychology but successfully recombined as *psychotechnics* during the war. On the basis of this military success, an amalgamation of European scientific research and US Taylorism became standard equipment of modern industrial management. The dream of a body without fatigue reached its sinister peak in the dictatorial regimes of the 1930s. The TB scare was key in the emerging bond between the body, the military, industry, and politics.

We can see this trajectory in architecture. Architects repeatedly used disease imagery to express concern for social order. Architecture's traditional role of imposing order takes on different meanings with different diseases. The reconfiguration of the medical body by new sciences leads to a reconfiguration of architecture. Take Le Corbusier. The opening pages of *Toward an Architecture* (1923) give his diagnosis of the state of architecture, condemning the traditional house for producing the debilitating effect of tuberculosis (consumption). He goes on to promote the healthy engineer over the unhealthy architect:

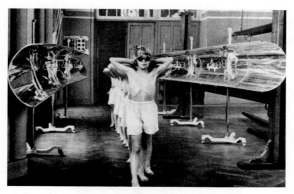

Children during heliotherapy session, 1937

We have become sedentary beings, that is our lot. The house eats away at us in our immobility, like consumption. We will soon need too many sanatoria.... Engineers are healthy and virile, active and useful, moral and joyful. Architects are disenchanted and idle, boastful or morose. That is because they will soon have nothing to do. *We have no more money* to pile up historical keepsakes. We need to cleanse ourselves.... The diagnosis is clear. Engineers make architecture.... People still believe, here and there, in architects, just as people blindly believe in doctors.[5]

Throughout the book, health is a battle cry. The final chapter opposes the healthy modern workplace to the unhealthy private house: "The machine that we live in is an old coach full of tuberculosis." Like so many architects, Le Corbusier expands the medical argument from the house to the city. In *Urbanisme* (1925) he opposes the fatiguing city and looks for a "cure," concluding that *"surgery"*↓ is required to remove the "cancer" of degenerate street layouts and "rotten old houses full of tuberculosis." He relates disease of the streets to the disease of the house. But while he associates the house with actual tuberculosis, the city is metaphorically cancerous.

In his film *L'Architecture d'aujourd'hui*↑ (1929), made in
collaboration with Pierre Chenal, Le Corbusier argues that
disease breeds in the city because in the twentieth century
people still live as if in the Middle Ages. He explicitly
equates disease with disorder in the city. His solution:
cut through the fabric of the old city and exercise on
the roof garden. The film's tour through his villas of the
1920s emphasizes once again the value of sunbathing and
exercise. It culminates in close-ups, shot on diagonal from
below, of a man and two women excitedly working out in
a kind of sexualized intensity on the roof garden of Villa
Church in exercise clothing and high heels. The house is
first and foremost a machine for health, a form of therapy.

Le Corbusier had long been obsessed with health. Arriving in Paris from his small hometown, La Chaux-des-Fonds in Switzerland, he complained about feeling exhausted all the time until he met Dr. Pierre Winter, who introduced him to exercise as a way of combating fatigue and stress. They played basketball together every week. Winter would become a contributor to *L'Esprit nouveau*, which regularly covered sporting events and informed its readers of new athletic records. In an article in *L'Esprit nouveau* called "Sports," Winter writes:

> Let us put our personal life and our social life in order. If everybody methodically studies his daily timetable with a view to taylorizing his acts and gestures ... if we all banished idle habits and lackadaisical work, wasted effort ... if sleep were better regulated ... when all those extra minutes were added up, one might find time for sport, for tending to the body, ... to regulate one's life is to control it and is a great source of deep joy. ... Sport introduces an element of ORDER in life.[6]

Winter was an enthusiast of the authoritarian wing of the syndicalist movement in France and a follower of Georges Valois (the self-proclaimed French Mussolini). In a 1926 article for Valois's journal on Le Corbusier's plan for a new kind of city, Winter writes: "Only a strong program of urbanism. The program of a Fascist government is capable of adapting the modern city to the needs of all." This intimate bond between architecture, urbanism, disease, war, industry, and politics is explicit throughout the work of Le Corbusier and many of his colleagues in the interwar period.

The intersection between design, medicine, and war keeps running through architectural discourse into the second half of the century. The Eameses' famous designs of the 1940s and 1950s, for example, are usually understood as reacting against the cold materials and forms of 1920s and 1930s furniture design that looked like doctor's equipment and as expressing a new concern for the body, for natural materials and organic forms. But there is nothing natural about the work. In fact, the Eames plywood chair is the result of medical and military research.

During World War II, Charles and Ray Eames had formed a company with John Entenza to mass-produce plywood war products. In 1941–42 they developed a molded plywood splint for the US Navy to replace a metal leg splint that did not sufficiently secure the leg and even led to gangrene and death. By the war's end, more than 150,000 *Eames splints↓* had been shipped to the Navy. The splint performed very well in the field and was praised for its lifesaving features. In addition, the company designed and developed a plywood body litter and an arm splint, molded plywood aircraft parts, etc. By 1945 the Eameses were producing molded plywood chairs with the technology they had developed for the military. A photograph of the plywood lounge chair

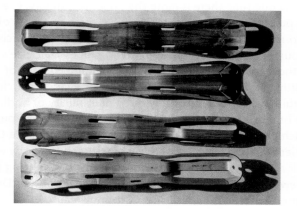

of 1946 shows Charles Eames reclining on it, the position of his leg indicating that he had not forgotten where it came from. In addition, the Eameses produced molded plywood children's furniture, *molded plywood animals*←, lightweight plywood cabinets, and even plywood Christmas decorations made out of leftover splints. Military and medical equipment had become the basis of domestic equipment.

For the Eameses, as for Le Corbusier, the designer is a surgeon. In the course of an interview Charles Eames said: "The preoccupation with self-expression is no more appropriate to the world of art than it is to the world of surgery. That does not mean I would reduce self-expression to zero; I am sure that really great surgeons operate on the edge of intuition. But the rigorous constraints in surgery – those are important in any art." Yet the Eameses' orthopedic body is not Le Corbusier's tuberculoid body. At any one time there is more than one such theory. Even the polemical pages of *L'Esprit nouveau* offer a number of theories of health: from Dr. Winter's hygiene and exercise through Dr. Allendy's homeopathy to Jaques-Dalcroze's rhythmic gymnastics. Each produced a unique image of the healthy body. The modern body housed by modern architecture was not a single body but a multiplicity of bodies. The body was no longer a stable point of reference around which an architecture could be built. Architects like Le Corbusier and his colleagues actively redesigned the body with their architecture rather than housing it or symbolizing it. A new spirit (*l'Esprit nouveau*) requires a new body, as Dr. Winter writes in his article "Le Corps nouveau":

A truly new spirit can only exist in a new body. Instinctively, modern man knows that.... We have to realize that the most formidable discovery of our time is *Health* understood in this more comprehensive sense. Physical health, basis of mental health, basis of every balanced activity, of all production, in all domains, and in that of art as much as in all the others.... The body will emerge naked in the sun, washed, muscled, supple.[7]

The body is not simply physical. *L'Esprit nouveau* was also obsessed with the relationship between psyche and body. It published articles by Dr. Allendy and his colleague Dr. Laforgue on the differences between Freudian psychoanalysis and French psychiatry with titles like "The Conscious and the Unconscious," "Neuroses," "Dreams," and "The Oedipus Complex." While Le Corbusier was sometimes dismissive of psychoanalysis, he repeatedly spoke of the intimate relationship between mind and body, portraying mental stability as the product of a healthy physical environment. In *Urbanisme* he argues that degeneration of the city leads to "physical and nervous sickness" and in *La Ville radieuse* he proposes that the new living cell be a machine for the "*Recuperation of physical and nervous energy* . . . the upkeep of the human machine: cleaning, draining the toxic substances, recuperating nervous energy, maintenance or increase of physical energy."[8]

If architectural discourse has from its beginning associated building and body, the body that it describes is the medical body, reconstructed by each new theory of health. Today, there are new instruments of medical diagnosis and new systems of architectural representation. Each implies new positions for design.

"Every age has its signature afflictions," Byung-Chul Han writes in *The Burnout Society*. We can add that each affliction has its architecture. The age of bacterial diseases – particularly tuberculosis – gave birth to modern architecture, to white buildings detached from the "humid ground where disease breeds," as Le Corbusier put it, smooth surfaces, big windows, and terraces to facilitate taking the sun and fresh-air cure. The discovery of antibiotics and particularly streptomycin in 1943 (the first antibiotic cure for tuberculosis) put an end to that age. In

the postwar years attention shifted to psychological problems. The same architects once concerned with the prevention of tuberculosis became obsessed with psychological problems. The architect was not seen just as a doctor but as a shrink, the house not just a medical device for the prevention of disease, but for providing psychological comfort, what Neutra called "nervous health."[9] The twenty-first century is, according to Han, the age of neurological disorders: depression, ADHD, borderline personality disorders, and burnout syndrome. What is the architecture of these afflictions? What does it mean for design?

The twenty-first century is also the age of allergies, the age of the "environmentally hypersensitive" unable to live in the modern world. Never at any one time in history have there been so many people allergic to chemicals, buildings, electromagnetic fields (EMF), fragrances.... Since the environment is now almost completely man-made, we have become allergic to ourselves, to our own hyperextended body in a kind of autoimmune disorder.

There are communities of the afflicted living in a kind of re-play of the 1960s in bubbles, tents, and old cars that have been "cleaned" of all toxic materials, usually in the desert or far away from civilization. Nomads moving at the very sniff of a chemical coming from a shifting wind that brings "whiffs of industry, detergent, fabric softener, fertilizers, pesticides, herbicides...exhaust from cars," as Dodie Bellamy puts it in "When the Sick Rule the World."[10] They are the dropouts of our age. On the other side of the spectrum, there is the "burnout society" that Han writes about. Those who in working for themselves push themselves harder than anybody could have pushed them, the achievement subject, who turns out to be much more disciplined than the obedience subject, despite the fact that he obeys only himself – master and slave conflated. No one can be so brutal with anybody as with oneself, pushing the limits of the imaginable, this creature does not experience it as pain or as obligation but as self-realization. The environmental hypersensitive are not mentioned by Han perhaps because he considers them, as many in the medical establishment do, afflicted by a neurological disorder: depressed or hypo-chondriac. The seemingly opposite symptoms might be two sides of the same coin.

Implied in all of this is a different city and new questions for design. Or very ancient questions about the limits of the body and mind, and how to take shelter in a threatening world.

The idea of the transparent human fully articulate in its likes and dislikes is a market-driven concept of an ideal consumer constantly offering feedback to reduce any friction in the production, distribution, and consumption of artifacts. If Freud says you can never know yourself, perhaps Amazon agrees, as its algorithm informs you that "people like you also bought x" before tweaking the algorithm in response to unexpected responses from people like you. *Human-centered* means "market-centered" in an age in which the market is not just for visible products but all the interconnected calculations of government, education, health, water, energy, finance, debt, copyright, genetics, and access. When the reach of the market is so massive and so comprehensive that it no longer seems to have an outside, human-centered design is ultimately not so interested in human well-being. What if design is precisely not human-centered? What if design is only design inasmuch as it challenges contemporary definitions of *human*?

"There ought to be recognition of precariousness as a shared condition of human life (indeed as a condition that links human and non-human animals) . . . Precariousness implies living socially, that is, the fact that one's life is always in some sense in the hands of the other. . . . I am already in the hands of the other when I try to take stock of who I am."

—Judith Butler

R. M. Schindler at his camping site, Yosemite.

9

HUMAN-CENTERED DESIGN

If the human is a question mark, *design* is a word for how that question is engaged. Design literally takes shape, makes shape, through the indeterminacy of the human. Or, to say it the other way around, there would be no concept of design if the human was something clear and stable.

Design projects an image of clarity – a crisply defined object, instrument, or space – precisely because things are not clear. Yet design discourse acts as if human needs and desires unproblematically organize design. *Human* is a magic word invoked to make design seem more ethical, sensitive, organic, responsive, and responsible. *Human* is always something positive and essential – as if we all already know what it is or have no fear of really knowing what it is.

Design is defense. Most theories of design present the human as under some kind of threat that needs to be urgently countered by design. The defense is seen to draw from some quality deeply embedded in the human, as if design itself is the natural human way to preserve the human. The most radical attempts to reshape the human are typically carried out under this guise of reinforcing and protecting the human. Design is a paradoxical gesture that changes the human in order to protect it.

Modern design discourse, in all its countless variations throughout the twentieth century, was all about a new world, a modernity that had to be given shape or whose hidden shape needed to be brought to the surface, including the shape of the "new human" corresponding to that world, a modern creature living a modern life enhanced by modern tools in modern spaces. Yet the discourse about this newly invented figure never stopped talking about the need to protect fundamental permanent "human needs," "human scale," "human nature," "human brain," "human soul," and so on. The new human was repeatedly advertised as a supercharged version of the very oldest human. Modern design was a double movement, connecting the future to the deepest past, as if the species was simply rebooting itself.

R. M. Schindler argued in his 1912 manifesto for "modern architecture" that the first ancient gestures of expanding human physical and psychological capacity with tools would inevitably grow into the ability to domesticate the whole planet:

> The feeling of security of our ancestor came in the seclusion and confinement of his cave. . . . The man of the future does not try to escape the elements. He will rule them. His home is no more a timid retreat: The earth has become his home. . . . The comfort of the dwelling lies in its complete control of space, climate, light, mood, within its confines.[1]

For Schindler, the house should be a kind of tent, a minimal shelter in an already tamed natural world. The evidence of the expansion of the human is the very lightness of modern design as a kind of camping equipment – what Eileen Gray would term *le style camping* when talking about her own *mobile furniture*↑ designed for her E1027 house of 1927 and the need for a new kind of domestic interior that addresses human needs. The modern mechanized world of calculation is unable to shelter the human. For Gray, the human has to be discovered again and the whole point of design is to offer this gesture of rediscovery to the users, who will paradoxically finally feel human in being at once extended and completed:

> We must rediscover the human being in plastic
> expression, the human intention that underlies
> material appearance and the pathos of this modern
> life, which has initially only been expressed in
> algebraic terms. . . . One must build for the human
> being that he might rediscover in the architectural
> construction the joys of self-fulfillment in a whole
> that extends and completes him.[2]

Eileen Gray and Jean Badovici, camping tent

Le Corbusier likewise presented modernity as a return to a primitive nomadic existence – the "modern nomad." He repeatedly spoke about the rebirth of the human body and brain. In *The Decorative Art of Today* (1925) he described design as an "orthopedic art," the prosthetic extension of the body with "artificial limbs."[3] The new body parts transform human capacity but need to be replaced whenever a better tool comes along in a continuous dramatic evolution of the species. They redesign human biology as "new organs awake in us." The tools themselves are "living beings, like a powerful or delicate species of animal of astounding ability." We have "bred a race" of machines to work for us and "machines beget machines" in a relentless evolution of technological capacity that seems miraculous and exceeds our understanding in a "dismaying complexity of organs." The experience of our hugely expanded body and brain is one of awe and vertigo in the face of a new nature – as if the human had conquered the natural world with technology only to be faced with the equally challenging new nature of technology itself. There is the palpable sense of having returned to "the place of genesis, where beings are remade."

Yet Le Corbusier insists that the human remains as the regulating constant at the heart of this overwhelming new ecology of artificial life-forms. The human is the essential "compass" of design and "to search for human scale, for human function, is to define human needs." The species is literally being remade in a radical transformation of its biology and mentality, yet the guiding reference point is still its very first gesture to invent the first artificial limbs to protect its vulnerable naked body to survive in the "inhuman (extra-human)" conditions of nature. In the face of the shock of modern industrialized life and the "disquiet that we no longer feel well adapted," Le Corbusier insists that "the client is a man, familiar to us all and precisely defined."

Le Corbusier repeatedly legitimized his work by telling stories about the first humans and never stopped insisting that his central concern was with reinforcing and protecting certain unchanging human qualities. His arguments are full of declarations about "human bases," "human problems," "human mind," "human satisfaction," "human resonances," "human spirit," "human fear," "human conscience," and so on. Untroubled by modesty, he prided himself on his ability to comprehend and address both the physiological needs of the human body and "the mysteries of human psychology," including especially "the fundamental questions which spring from the very depths of human feelings." The human is treated as something fundamental, a given with physiological, emotional, and intellectual needs to be addressed by design. It is an ancient creature that doesn't suddenly find itself within modernity as if getting off a bus in a shockingly dense and rapidly moving metropolis.

Rather, it is a self-modernizing creature always enveloped in projections generated from within itself. *The Decorative Art of Today* argues that the rapid reinvention of the human by technology should be embraced precisely because technology is itself human. Indeed, nothing is more human than technology. Human inventions are ruthlessly tested by the humans who gave birth to them, even when that invention is the human itself:

> The human factor remains intact, since the machine was invented by man to serve human needs; that is the significant and stable element: the machine is conceived within the spiritual framework which we have constructed for ourselves.[4]

The discourse of modern design repeatedly argued that the human can regulate its ever more radical transformation of itself by reference back to the beginning of self-design with the invention of the first tools and ornaments. The claim that human artifacts are organic parts of the body – that technology is biology – is an obsessive mantra of designers, theorists, and teachers.

For Hannes Meyer, for example, "building is a biological process." His 1926 text on *"The New World"*→ described the transformative effect of the total "mechanization of our planet ... the victory of man the thinker over amorphous nature ... that gives our new world its shape." [5] Nothing is what it was. Machines have expanded bodily and brain functions. Homes have become mobile. People no longer have a homeland. The house is not just a machine for living but a "living machine" for the "semi-nomad." Meyer repeated parts of this text when becoming director of the Bauhaus in 1928, describing the house as the design of a "biological apparatus serving the needs of body and mind." He called for an ever more precise set of measurements at the intersection of human and building physiology – testing the interrelationships between human beings, animals, and environment. But this figure to be analyzed scientifically is not radically transformed by the new technological environment. Meyer is even concerned with measuring its interaction with the garden, reconnecting it with domesticated nature. Underneath all the change is a more primitive humanity, such that the modernity of design is not to be judged in the aesthetic effect but in "its direct relationship to human existence."[6]

Buckminster Fuller likewise saw design as the scientific project of providing shelter for the human by engaging directly with its biology. His 1938 investigation of the question "what is man?" argued that not only is the human body and brain inseparable from its "prosthetic" extensions with technologies but that the human body

Hannes Meyer, Co-op Zimmer

Inventions d'Or'mo

was itself the first tool, a technology that can and should be modified.[7] Max Bill likewise *argued→* in 1948 there is no real difference between machines and handcraft because "these are simply the prostheses we create to implement our work."[8] To see modern design as an organic extension of human capacities was an orthodoxy of modern design rather than a polemical position. The original capacity to invent, to design prosthetic artifacts with the first tools and first words, becomes the very figure of modernization.

But this common line of thinking also raised the possibility that the negative effects of technology are inherently human and can likewise be traced back to the very first tools. Richard Neutra's *Survival through Design* (1954) even zoomed in on the uniquely expanded brain that originally enabled the human to become "human" through invention, noting that it "harbors trouble":

> In human design, we could conceivably see organic evolution continued, and extending into a man-shaped future. At any rate, that phenomenally intensive development in the multilayered cortex

of the human upper brain had not yet with certainty been proved a blind alley or a dismal failure. To be sure, this distinctly human brain harbors trouble, but it also may furnish some as yet untried survival aids.[9]

Neutra argued that other animals with a lesser brain survive by gradually adjusting themselves over long biological ages, but the human is a tinkerer who "may perish by his own explosive and insidious inventions." Humanity is being victimized by its own artifacts and is defenseless against its self-destruction. The species is "strangled and suffocated by our own design" and running out of time. Yet Neutra held out hope that returning design to its original physiological and mental origins with a more subtle and circumspect concept of design could open a different path. The harsh conditions faced by earliest man are a paradise in comparison to the violence of contemporary artificial nature. Neutra developed an extended physiological and psychological portrait of the human organism, starting with the extreme ecological thought that all organisms are not easily distinguished from each other or from the environment since they live on and in each other in a continuous chemical fusion. The basic question he asked is "whether the human race is fatefully self-destructive" or can survive "by our own design."

In all these arguments that attempt to naturalize modern design by appeal to the origins of humanity, some kind of gap between the human and its designs is seen to have produced a kind of biological, psychological, and intellectual crisis that the designer needs to address by recalling how the whole process began. There is a survival crisis that uncannily echoes the very beginnings of design.

Cover of *A* magazine, edited by Bo Bardi, Zevi and Pagani, 1946

In 1958 Lina Bo Bardi even argued that in the age of artificial satellites orbiting above us the very origin of the human needs to be redesigned. Our self-destructiveness goes back to our first "startled" reaction to our own artifacts:

> Man increasingly dominates nature – he knows the composition of matter and roams through space – but he remains "ancient," still thinking along ancient lines, acting in ancient ways, and staring up on the fruits of his labors with the same startled eyes he did thousands of years ago. And that fruit? – the prospect of self-destruction, the yawning chasm that has opened up between technical and scientific achievement and the human capacity to think.[10]

Bo Bardi calls for the species to finally abandon its antiquity, to "build his humanity anew" with a recognition of human problems and human rights and a new understanding of technology that will enable humans to tame the very mechanism that they have created and will inevitably destroy them. Prehistory becomes the battlefield of the future.

Sigfried Giedion, who since the mid-1920s had been the leading promoter of modern architecture as the naturalization of the industrialized world, had second thoughts in the face of mechanized slaughter in World War II. His remarkable *Mechanization Takes Command*→ (1948) analyzes the history of the anonymous industrial design of everyday objects as the history of a destructive intrusion of mechanization into every dimension of the life, biology, and mentality of the human. It argued that mechanization is all the more dangerous and difficult to control precisely because it "sprang entirely from the mind of man." Our interior is more difficult to control than our exterior. Giedion argued that the human organism is a constant but its relationship to the environment is unstable, continually changing, and self-threatening. The book begins by arguing that basic human values have to be reinstated yet ends by calling for a new type of man. The concluding prescription for this "new man" finishes with the plaintive call: "It is time that we become human again."[11] Once again the new is old and the old is new. The future lies in the deep past. Symptomatically, *Giedion*↙ spent the next decade going

to the archaeological sites of the oldest known human artifacts and finally produced two huge volumes on the prehistoric origin of art and architecture. *The Eternal Present: The Beginnings of Art*, the first of the two, begins by restating that "It is time that we became human again."[12]

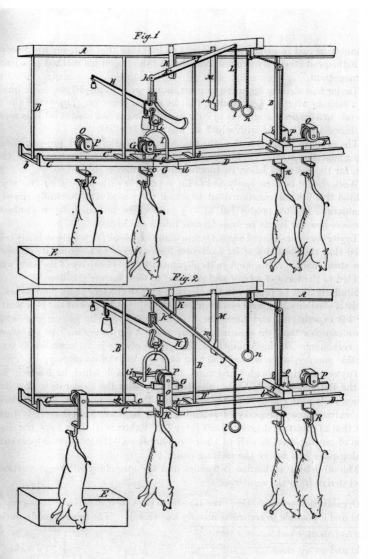

Fig.1

Fig.2

Faustkeil
Handaxe

Kandiszuckerbrecher
Rock candy breaker

Kombinationshammer
Combination hammer

Chirurgenhammer
Surgeon's mallet

Schusterhammer
Shoemaker's hammer

Treibhammer
Embossing hammer

Kleiner Vorschlaghammer
Small sledge hammer

Schmiedehammer
Blacksmith's hammer

Bildhauerhammer
Sculptor's hammer

Maurerhammer
Bricklayer's hammer

Hammer eines Kabellegers
Lineman's hammer

Elektrikerhammer
Electrician's hammer

Feilenhauerhammer
File-maker's hammer

Astronautenhammer
Astronaut's hammer

Bildhauerschlegel
Sculptor's hammer

Indianischer Hammer
American Indian hammer

Elektrikerhammer
Electrician's mallet

Tapeziererhammer
Upholsterer's tack hammer

Hufschmiedhammer
Farrier's hammer

Hammer für Rohleder
Rawhide mallet

Blechniethammer
Tinner's riveting hammer

Hammer mit Kugelfinne
Ballpeen hammer

Steinmetzhammer
Stonecutter's hammer

Zimmererschlegel
Carpenter's mallet

This return to the origins of the human is not simply an organizing principle of modern design. It is the tradition of most design theory. The oldest surviving text of Western design theory by Vitruvius famously turns on his account of the original discovery of fire, language, tools, and architecture. The whole tradition of classical architectural theory was based on endlessly revisiting that scene. Leon Battista Alberti, Vincenzo Scamozzi, Cesare Cesariano, Fra Giocondo, William Chambers, Claude Perrault, Marc-Antoine Laugier, Quatremère de Quincy, Viollet le-Duc, Gottfried Semper, to name but a few, all carefully paint their own portrait of the primal scene.[13] Modern architects inevitably joined in, as did those challenging them. Bernard Rudofsky's *Architecture Without Architecture* (1965) speculated that architecture began when humans imitated the shelters of apes.[14] Hans Hollein's *Man TransFORMS←* (1976) talks about the crucial invention of the hand axe.[15] And so on. Each design theory has a slightly different account of the origin of humanity depending on its particular philosophy, reconstructing the original scene in order to reinforce a key dimension of their polemic. Each presents itself as restoring the human but it is never the same human that is being restored.

It is hard to find a design theorist who doesn't at some point return to the primal scene of the very birth of design. But the real paradox is that this scene is supposed to demonstrate what is supposedly self-evident: what makes the human human. Design is a defense of the human but what is being defended is never clear.

The nineteenth-century dream of "total design" has been realized. The famous slogan of the 1907 Deutscher Werkbund "from the sofa cushion to city planning," updated in 1952 with Ernesto Rogers's "from the spoon to the city," now seems far too modest when the patterns of atoms are being carefully arranged and colossal artifacts, like communication nets, encircle the planet. Designers have become role models in the worlds of science, business, politics, innovation, art, and education but paradoxically they have been left behind by their own concept. They remain within the same limited range of design products and do not participate fully in the expanded world of design. Ironically, this frees them up to invent new concepts of design.

"The grand attempt to make industrial design a motor for renewing society as a whole has failed – an appalling indictment of the perversity of a system."

–Lina Bo Bardi

Hand with mutilated fingers at Gargas
in Sigfried Giedion, *The Eternal Present:
The Beginnings of Art*

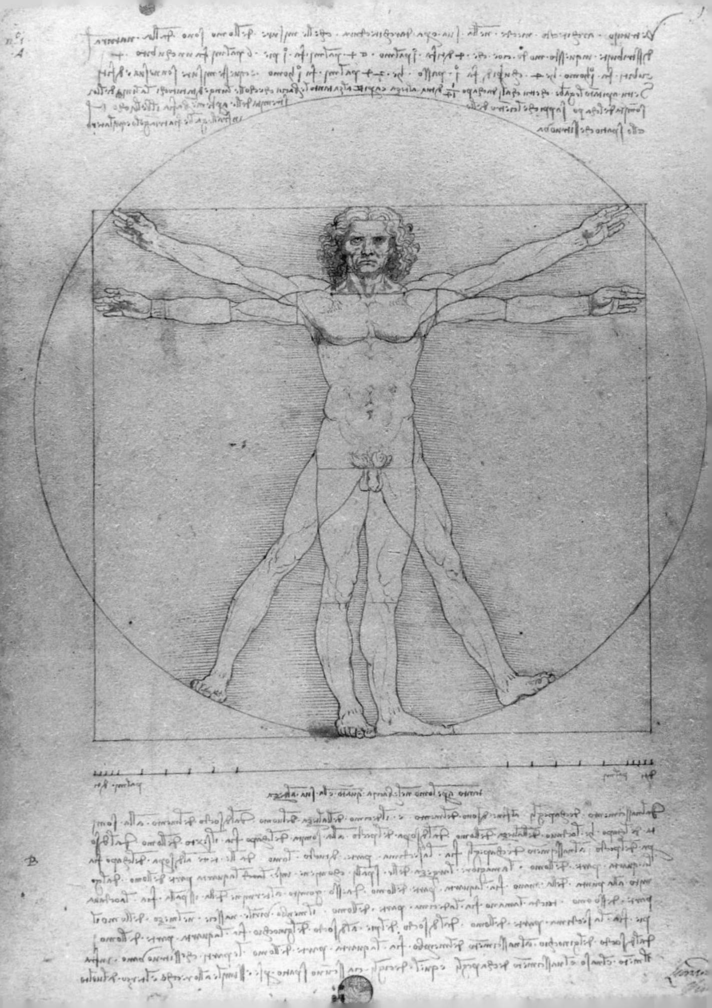

10

THE FRICTIONLESS SILHOUETTE

Each theory that locates the human at the center of design actually reinvents the human while acting as if it were always there.

This attempt to naturalize the reinvented human is often portrayed in polemical images of a solitary figure surrounded by webs of design. All the diversity, mystery, complications, and strangeness of the human is replaced with a single smooth silhouette. The very things seen to be all too human – psychology, voice, face, expression, breathing, temperature, rhythm, asymmetry, sweat, porosity, breathing, fluctuations, awkwardness – disappear in favor of a single confident line marking the exterior limit of the human.

The canonic Western image of the human at the center of design is Leonardo's 1490 drawing of *Vitruvian Man*← immersed in the geometric order of the circle and square. It is meant to demonstrate that the geometry of the cosmos is already embedded in the proportions of the "well shaped man" that has been "designed by nature" as Vitruvius had put it in the oldest surviving text of Western architectural theory.[1] The naked figure has no ground other than the surrounding geometry in which it is suspended. It is ambiguous as to whether the geometry is being defined by the figure's movements or is confining the figure, whether it is radiating design as its first clothing or is forced to stand in the circle or stand in the square. If anything, the geometry appears as a constraint. Far from a given, this figure of the human is manufactured in a complex exchange in which it is being disciplined, even imprisoned, by the geometry that supposedly emerges from it. The default human is alone, white, male, athletic – a highly ideological fantasy figure presented as the norm, a model human on which all architectural design will be based.

The classical architecture based on this model is meant to be a kind of mirror in which the human sees itself perfected. Vitruvius argues that the proportions of "perfect buildings" are based on the proportions of the body (along with the system of measurements and mathematics itself). To look at this architecture will supposedly be to feel the cosmic resonances of the universe that are embedded in the proportions of the ideal human body, but not in one's own less-perfect body. The proportions are ideal precisely because they cannot be found in any one example in the world. Design offers the self-reflection of an improved body.

The use of an ideal body to generate a proportional system is not simply a Western concept. Ancient Egyptian art, for example, used a *proportional system*↓ for generating perfect

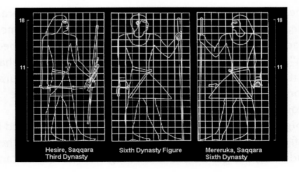

Hesire, Saqqara
Third Dynasty

Sixth Dynasty Figure

Mereruka, Saqqara
Sixth Dynasty

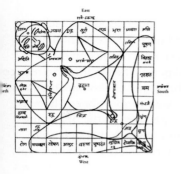

bodies based on a grid of units with eighteen units to the all-important top of the forehead. Both the real and the ideal body were unstable. Bodies grew significantly in size with the development of intense agriculture and at a certain point the ideal system was also abruptly changed. In the *Vastu Shastra*↑, the Sanskrit treatises on design developed between six thousand and three thousand years ago, the body is again both microcosm and macrocosm, a system that ultimately determines the location, function, height, and even sequence of construction for every element of a temple or a family house. A silhouetted male body appears within a geometric order that at once comes from the body and entraps it. Yet the orchestrating body is not always male. In Malaysia and Indonesia, for example, the Ilmu Taju system for design uses the *depa*, the matriarch's arm span, as the determining element for proportioning all building elements to maintain well-being. Countless examples across diverse cultures and times portray a human figure linking health, religion, cosmology, and design.

Leonardo's iconic image of the human at once suspended in and disciplined by its own geometry was self-consciously echoed in twentieth-century images of diagrammatic human silhouettes suspended in the geometry of ergonomic calculations – most obviously in the drawings by Ernst Neufert in the 1930s and Henry Dreyfuss in the 1950s – that were offered to designers as a source of standardized measures to calibrate the physical settings for any human activity. The most republished and influential design books of all, these manuals are found in every design studio. The cosmic human has been displaced by the human understood as a technical instrument made of coordinated parts whose motion needs to be as integrated into the mechanics of the home as it would be in any vehicle or workplace. The ambition to reduce any sense of friction between body and environment remains. The measurements of a naked, "well-proportioned" human and the movements of its limbs are given at the beginning of the manuals with an image of a body that stands still facing the reader – like a stationary athlete before an event. Its outlined naked "normal" body is encased only in its own geometry but inside the book it is dressed and encased in the geometry of spaces and equipment for work, domestic life, rest, and play as it energetically carries out every conceivable activity. The purpose of the books is to synchronize the geometry of the body to that of the spaces it engages with, using the body's movements to design space. It is as if the body is carving its habitat. All the measurements of the body are now given to all the spaces, furnishing, and equipment that the body makes contact with. Human dimensions become the dimensions of the designed world. The body that will seamlessly occupy that world is a schematic silhouette, the minimal outline of a figure that is becoming itself in absorbing or expanding itself with design.

Neufert's self-conscious echo of the Leonardo drawing, with another standing naked male figure sweeping its arms to

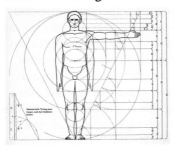

draw ideally proportioned geometry, first appeared on the cover his 1935 publication *Der Mensch als Mass und Ziel* (Man as measure and goal) – a title that already hints at the ambivalence about whether man is to be the model for design or the target to be

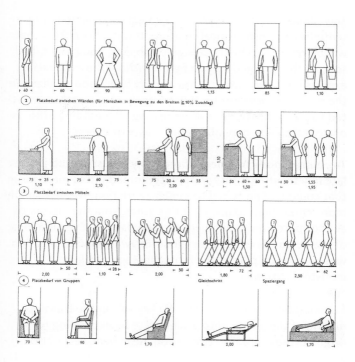

(2) Platzbedarf zwischen Wänden (für Menschen in Bewegung zu den Breiten ≥ 10% Zuschlag)

(3) Platzbedarf zwischen Möbeln

(4) Platzbedarf von Gruppen · Gleichschritt · Spaziergang

designed.[2] The figure has some definition of muscles, hair, genitals, face and even eyes looking away. But in the following pages this "normal" figure becomes a *faceless dressed silhouette*↑ portrayed earnestly standing, sitting, walking, working, sleeping, eating, exercising, entering, leaving, greeting, and reading. *Bau-Entwurfslehre*, the much larger definitive version of Neufert's book, appeared the following year with the same opening drawing now *defining even more detailed proportions*← following the golden section and the same introductory text on "man as measure and goal" followed by additional drawings of the activities of cleaning, washing, schooling, drawing, drinking, riding horses, milking, swimming, and changing.[3]

This silhouette of the human is a constructed artifact presented as a transhistorical creature. It is itself a design that will be reinforced by the design of objects, equipment, and spaces. The outlined human figure without muscles, facial expression, or eccentricity has already been industrialized in the pages of these books. It is everywhere earnestly committed to productivity, even when resting. The guiding ethos is one of efficiency, minimizing any waste of energy.

The human body had been thoroughly industrialized in the late nineteenth-century workplace, turned into a mechanism that could be fine-tuned to minimize friction. Neufert simply represented the expansion of this ethos from the factory to all the spaces and equipment of everyday life. Even the idea of the human as a faceless silhouette awaiting optimization was an integral part of the biotechnological regime of industrialization.

Étienne-Jules Marey had played a key role in the transformation of the human into a silhouette by expanding his original study of blood circulation, heartbeat, respiration, and muscles in the 1860s to the movements of humans and other animals in his series of books starting with *La machine animale* in 1873.[4] He insisted that the animal organism was not fundamentally different than that of a machine and developed techniques in the early 1880s for showing human movement in which the body was abstracted into a silhouette by a white suit or into lines drawn on a black suit with the face masked. The research had already inspired an array of scientists in Europe, along with the photographer Eadweard Muybridge in the United States. Marey had even recommended that Muybridge use silhouettes on a revolving wheel to produce the illusion of movement before later criticizing him for producing no more than a silhouette in his photographs of movement – showing the outline of motion

but not its anatomy. The abstracted figure had traveled
to the United States as Frederick Winslow Taylor
developed his time-motion technique in the 1890s for
further refining the human organism into an ever more
efficient machine and the machine into an ever more
responsive organism – a technique that would become
hugely influential internationally after it was first
published in 1911.[5] Taylor's only interest in the body
was to maximize output in a series of ever more efficient
actions. In 1914 the *cyclographs*↓ of Frank and Lillian
Gilbreth made movement itself the protagonist as a
white line of motion against a dark background with the
human organism becoming an even more ghostly figure,
a blur supporting the clearly defined white trace.

In Russia, Aleksei Gastev pursued the Gilbreths' photographic methods relentlessly in his Central Institute of Labor. He argued in 1921 that the world of the machine "is giving birth to its own types of people" that must be accepted and called for "a rather bold design of human psychology."[6] The scientific attempt to find the perfect shape of movement for each task had to be matched by a new psychology of the human that was equally precisely adjusted to support the repetition of that movement. This psychology was ultimately that of the machine itself in an age in which the machines are the real managers.

After the horror of World War I, the "new man" that had already been standardized into an efficient machine part was increasingly portrayed as a traumatizing and traumatized automaton, whether it be as a biotechnical hybrid of flesh and technology or a faceless mannequin. George Grosz's painting *The New Man* ↙ (1921), for example, portrays the blank head of the engineer with his drawing

machine and exercise equipment. The figure is smoothed into geometric shapes like the room itself, the equipment, and even the engineering drawing on the easel. The round head, round punching ball, and round engine part are aligned in an uncanny fusion of the no-longer-human human and design. In a sense, the damaged human figure is rebuilt in the smooth image of the machine.

A similar figure emerged at the same time in the drawings of Oskar Schlemmer as he reacted to his own trauma in the war by self-consciously reviving the study of human proportion and designing geometric humans. These silhouetted figures would become the core of his course *Der Mensch* at the Bauhaus.[7] In 1921 Schlemmer, who had been in and out of hospital during the war with two injuries, saw his work on the redesigned human body in terms of his own thoughts of being seriously physically and mentally

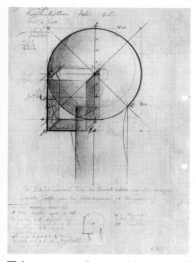

wounded as a soldier, and the sense that he "was not the same man who had volunteered." He explained why he had recently joined the faculty by observing that Gropius was taking the school beyond traditional education by rebuilding the human: "the Bauhaus is 'building' something quite different from what was planned – human beings."[8]

This construction project started with the lives of the students themselves and expanded out to the networks of industrialization. With Schlemmer, the human form becomes pure geometry, as exemplified by his technique for producing the most minimal drawing of the *human head* using a square and circle and through his dances, in which the body itself becomes a smooth mannequin embedded in geometric figures. The most influential school of modern design was organized around the reshaping of the body into a designed artifact.

Not by chance, Ernst Neufert had been one of the first students of Walter Gropius at the Bauhaus in 1919 and worked in the office of Gropius on the new Bauhaus building in Dessau. He became deeply committed to the Bauhaus project to define the "Normalmensch" as a model for standardization of design. He envisaged a complete empire of standardization supposedly emerging out the ideal proportions of the body but in reality disciplining the body according to particular ideals. The approach resonated seamlessly with the fascist cult of the heroic perfected body, and Neufert became an integral part of the regime, responsible for standardization of industrial architecture in the Third Reich since 1939; yet the thirty-nine successive German editions of his book and translations into more than thirty languages are still used today as the standard reference on standards and is arguably the single most-used book in design. His little silhouetted figures have dispersed themselves across the planet as a kind of army of engineers busily shaping the designed world.

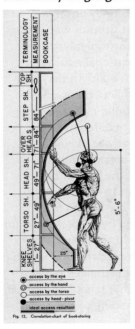

Fig. 12. Correlation-chart of book-storing

Neufert's figures were not alone. In 1939 Frederick Kiesler published his theory of design as "biotechnique," with his own version of the Vitruvian impulse to use the human body to dimension architecture to remove any "maladjustment" between human and environment.[9] Once again, the arc of the moving hands of a male body carves out an architecture perfectly fitted to the *body*↖. In

1941 the third edition of *Architectural Graphic Standards*, the American manual of standardized dimensions, included a set of drawings of "dimensions of the human figure" that had first been published in a 1934 article in an architectural journal. They showed a blackened silhouetted "average" male figure in a range of postures from standing, reaching, crawling, and crouching to sitting.

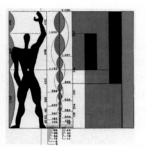

In 1943 Le Corbusier opportunistically responded to the occupation government's call for standardization in the building industry by starting to develop his own system for dimensioning the whole designed environment on the basis of an idealized "normal" male body. Once again the image of *standing male silhouette with a raised arm↑* defines a set of rules with "a grid designed to fit the man placed within it" based on the golden section. Le Corbusier insisted all architecture from all cultures from prehistoric times onwards have been based on such measurement "tools" taken from the body: "linked to the human person...an integral part of the human body."[10] Yet again, the human figure was both the model and the target with "a common measure capable of ordering the dimensions of that which contains and that which is contained." In fact, the geometry was developed for two years before the "human value" of the height was decided to be 1.75 m but then numbers didn't work out elegantly, and this "French" height was suddenly adjusted to 1.8288 m to match the more "English" height of 6 feet. The decision was not based on the height of the supposedly average body. On the contrary, the height of the average body was determined by the elegance of the mathematics.

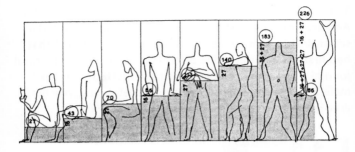

If, as Le Corbusier argued, all the manufactured objects to be dimensioned by designers are either the "*containers* of man or *extensions* of man," the first thing to get dimensioned is "man" itself. The faceless silhouetted figure that starts to sit, stand, lean, and stretch in Le Corbusier's *drawings↑* is a designer body that keeps getting adjusted. The proportional system was used by a group of Le Corbusier's colleagues to analyze *diagrammatic Muslim men↙* in the largest shantytown of Algiers in 1953. When Le Corbusier wanted to demonstrate that the system could be reconciled

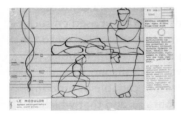

with the ancient Egyptian system in 1954, he was annoyed when his assistant drew the human figure as a woman, yet published it in his second book on his proportional system.[11]

The industrial designer Henry Dreyfuss published his own versions of the Leonardo drawing in 1955 with the silhouetted figures of woman and children now joining the male in defining a geometric space with the movements of their arms and legs. Average Joe was joined by Josephine and Joe Jr. with all their respective measurements. Dreyfuss had noticed during the war an uncanny echo of Leonardo's drawing in his own drawing of a tank driver with all the measurements for the reach of arms and legs to the controls arrayed around the figure. He started to redraw this schematic figure with ever more precise measurements as the basis for "human engineering." The epigraph of *Designing for People*, his first book in 1955, explicitly described design as the removal of friction between humans and the manufactured objects they encounter: "When the point of contact between the product and the people becomes a point of friction, then the industrial designer has failed."[12] Drawing all the dimensions of the body's movements will smooth its encounter with the world. The goal is to have "filled the gaps between human behavior and machine design." The book begins with the obligatory portrait of the prehistoric origin of design. For Dreyfuss, design began with the construction of a bowl that echoed the shape of the cupped hands used to drink water from a pool: "Intuitively, this prehistoric man was following the same principles of utility that today's industrial designer who creates for mass production." Dreyfuss saw his role as reuniting the designer with the vulnerable human. The role of the designer is to ease the

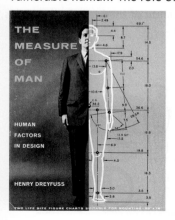

physical and psychological pressures of being completely surrounded by technologies.

In the series of editions of his 1959 book *The Measure of Man*, with its symptomatic subtitle *Human Factors in Design*, Dreyfuss would eventually increase the range of body types *to include aging, thinness, obesity, disability, and finally race↓*.[13] His drawings replaced the section on human dimensions in *Architectural Graphic Standards* from 1981 on, and the successive editions of Neufert's manual portrayed a more diverse human figure as a response in a kind of transatlantic warfare of abstract bodies. The sheer range of activities carried out by this global army of silhouettes kept multiplying – to such an extent that these ever-larger manuals could be reverse-engineered to provide an anthropological encyclopedia of what humans are doing. Yet the image of a normative transhistorical and transcultural figure still remained. This body that crosses national and cultural boundaries and occupies every workplace, street, vehicle, furniture, equipment, interface, social space, and private space is still just an outline, a schematic figure without expression or character – an engineered human.

Other versions of a silhouetted normative body surrounded by a geometry seen to come from within it arrived with the images of the human inside cybernetic feedback loops that echo those inside the human nervous systems in 1950s, *life-support plumbing for astronauts↗* whose complexity mirrors all the tubes inside the human in the 1960s, energy flows between the inside and the outside of the body in the 1980s, and biofeedback circuits today.

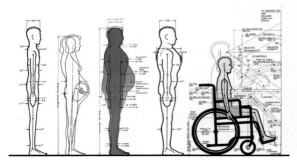

160

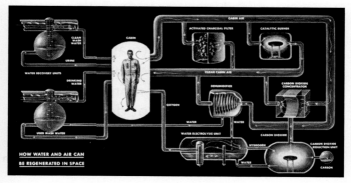

"Keeping Alive in Space: A Report from General Dynamics"

All these very different paradigms remove of any sense of stress between the human and its surroundings. Despite the dramatic upgrading of human capacity, design is seen to echo and amplify the human, as distinct from being a restraint, corrective, disguise, or replacement.

In every case, there is a disciplining of the body that is implicitly contrasted to the endless everyday personal refashioning of the body through clothes, makeup, shaving, haircuts, manicures, ornaments, diet, posture, gait, and exercise. The smooth line of the silhouette takes over from the unstable limit of the body constantly worked on in everyday life. The silhouette that represents the human takes over that space of self-reconstruction with the image of a new normal body. It is as if the design of equipment and spaces is offered as the improved form-fitting clothing of this figure. But the basic figure, the schematic outline, is itself the product of design. The figure seemingly waiting for design is never innocent. It has been designed.

Designers are always understood as solving a problem. Artists, intellectuals, and writers are expected to ask questions, to make us hesitate, to see our world and ourselves differently for a moment, and therefore to think. Why not design as a way of asking questions?

Why not design that produces thought-provoking hesitations in the routines of everyday life rather than simply servicing those routines? Why not design that encourages us to think? Design as an urgent call to reflect on what we and our companion species have become?

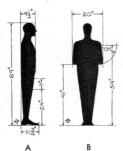

A

B

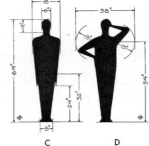

C

D

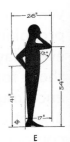

E

G

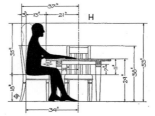

H

I

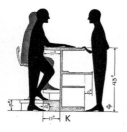

K

L

M

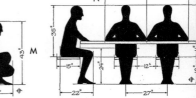

N

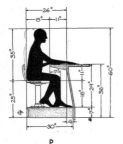

P

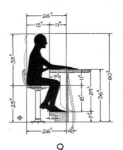

Q

S

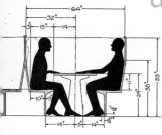

"When humanists accuse people of 'treating humans like an object,' they are thoroughly unaware that they are treating objects unfairly."

–Bruno Latour

11

DESIGNING
THE BODY

Modern architecture presented itself as lean
and fit, all the excess weight of neoclassical
tradition stripped off to reveal a muscular
and agile body in a white sports outfit.

The modern house was understood as a piece of exercise
equipment designed to produce a strong and healthy
body. Think of all the bodybuilding houses in modern
architecture: from Marcel Breuer's *apartment for gymnastics
teacher Hilde Levi in Berlin*← (1930), to Walter Gropius's
gym in his apartment for the German Building Exhibition
in Berlin (1931), to Richard Döcker's rooftop gym at
the Weissenhofsiedlung in Stuttgart (1927), to the
1,000-meter running track that Le Corbusier proposed for
the roof of his Immeuble Villas (1922). The athletic figure
is the paradigmatic client of modern architecture, or its
desired outcome. Modern architecture was a machine for
enhancing the body.

Not by chance, Rem Koolhaas choose the Downtown Athletic Club as the core of his "retroactive manifesto" of Manhattan in *Delirious New York* (1978). Less well known is his *Casa Palestra*↓, a bodybuilding house in the form of a Barcelona Pavilion "bent" to fit the curve of its allotted

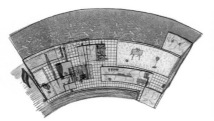

site within the exhibition hall of the 1986 Milan Triennale. The project, designed with OMA, was an homage to the Barcelona

Pavilion but also to modern architecture, under attack in those years as "lifeless, empty and puritanical": "It has always been our conviction that modern architecture is a hedonistic movement, that its abstraction, rigor and severity are in fact plots to create the most provocative settings for the experiment that is modern life."[1]

The newly curved Barcelona Pavilion is inhabited by gymnasts, bodybuilders, and exercise equipment in a sensuous explosion of projected images, lighting effects, and lasers. George Kolbe's bronze sculpture *Alba* (Dawn), originally placed by Mies van der Rohe at the end of the small water basin and *reflected in the water*↙, has been replaced with a 1983 Robert Mapplethorpe *photograph of Lisa Lyon*↓, the first Women's Bodybuilding champion. A new manifesto results from the tweaking of an old one. The supposedly calming space of Mies was turned into an erotics of exercise. Koolhaas, who wrote a script for an erotically charged film (*The White Slave*) before becoming an architect, turns architecture into a movie set for an expanding, eroticized body. The project takes modern architecture's dream of a buff body to a new level. Koolhaas positioned himself here in relationship to the time, the height of postmodernism and its attack on modern architecture, through a twisting of Mies that unleashes the sensuality of modern architecture that has been repressed by the discourse.

Adolf Koch's socialist body culture school, Lake Motzen, near Berlin

Take R. M. Schindler and Richard Neutra, well known in the history of modern architecture for their respective "health houses" for Doctor Phillip Lovell in California: Schindler's Lovell Beach house in Newport Beach (1922–26) and Neutra's town house in Los Angeles (1927–29). Less known is that the impulse behind both houses came less from straight modern architecture theories than from sex, health, psychoanalysis, and nudism theories. Modern architecture was here inseparable from a new lifestyle, which included a vegetarian diet, exercise, sunbathing in the nude, sleeping in the open air, and dressing in simple robes made with natural fibers. Many of these ideas came from the late nineteenth-century *Lebensreform* (Life reform) movement in Germany, which advocated a back-to-nature

lifestyle of fresh air, gardening, health food, alternative medicine, nudism, sexual liberation, and the avoidance of alcohol, tobacco, and vaccines. The ideas had arrived in California, where many proponents of the movement had emigrated. Neutra even contributed to the magazine *Nude Living* ← on the recommendation of his secretary Audrey Hardy, who was featured in its pages.

Pauline Schindler and Leah Lovell, "school in the garden"

Dr. Lovell was a naturopath and drugless practitioner who thought all diseases had a dietary origin. He never studied medicine but his theories of diet, exercise, sun therapy, and open-air sleeping were very influential in Southern California. He wrote a column for the *Los Angeles Times* entitled "Care of the Body" (the publisher of the newspaper, Harry Chandler, was one of his patients). The Lovell Houses of Schindler and Neutra were organized around his full regime of sun, air, exercise, fasting, and diet strategies. The Health house of Neutra, in particular, became a public demonstration of Lovell's theories, with en suite sleeping porches outside every room, "nude sunbathing opportunities" throughout the house, "hydrotherapy equipment" and "marathon showers" in the master bathroom, which was also equipped with a "built-in enema fixture with various douches and nozzles devices, thermostatically controlled."[2] Lovell opened the house to the public for two weekends, announcing it in his newspaper column, which included photographs, a description of the house, and a map showing how to get there. Around 15,000 people showed up and Neutra himself gave the tours. A photograph of the Lovell house appears in this column alongside ads for treating "sagging flabby

CARE OF THE BODY

The Home Built for Health

By Philip M. Lovell, N. D.

Author of "Diet for Health" and "The Health of the Child"

For years I have periodically written articles telling you how to build your home so that you can derive from it the maximum degree of health and beauty service. I have written on miscellaneous problems such as lighting, heating, hydrotherapy equipment, labor-saving devices, sleeping porches, material for construction and other health features. Always at the end of each article was the thought, "If I ever build a home myself—"

At last the day has arrived. We have built such a home—a home premised on the fundamental health principles and construction ideas which I have presented in my writings in the past.

Front View of Dr. Lovell Home of Health.

I know that there are many who are interested, and with this in mind we are opening it for public inspection before furnishing and occupying it.

Hence, consider this an invitation for all Care of the Body readers to visit this newly-constructed home built for health. It is located at 4616 Dundee Drive, Los Angeles, in the Los Felis hills adjacent

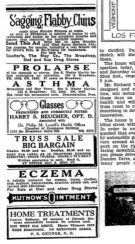

to Griffith Park. The accompanying sketch will show the way of getting there.

The house will be open for public inspection today, Sunday, the 15th inst., and Saturday and Sunday, the 21st and 22nd inst., respectively, from 8 a.m. to 5 p.m.

Mr. Richard T. Neutra, architect who designed and supervised the construction, will lecture at 3 p.m. on each of these days on building the home for health and will conduct the audience from room to room and place to place, describing in detail the purposes of each innovation.

The home is located at the end of a blind street with a wide turning radius. In order to avoid confusion it is requested that everyone visiting the house by automobile go to the end of the road, turn around at the turning basin and park on the right curb with your car facing downhill. I shall also ask that you please drive slowly and carefully on Dundee Drive, as there will probably be many people coming and going and

there are several blind turns.

For those who cannot inspect this home, a brief description will not be amiss.

The main construction is steel, built on a deep, reinforced concrete foundation. The walls, floors, ceilings and roof are all steel-girded, being covered with fireproof expanded steel and plaster.

The window sashes are steel and there is a greater profusion of them than in any home I have ever seen.

There are plenty of opportunities throughout the house for nude sun baths privately taken for each member.

Many of the windows are of the latest invention of glass, admitting ultra-violet light.

The bathrooms are completely equipped with hydrotherapy equipment, including such things as sitz baths, multiple marathon showers and the latest type of sanitary fixtures.

Sanitation and hygiene are the keynote.

The ventilation, sunshine and light ideas are exceedingly modern.

The bedrooms are built "en suite"; that is, every inside bedroom has its accompanying sleeping porch so that all sleeping can be done outdoors.

The lighting is indirect—mostly recessed inside the ceiling—and shows behind ribbed glass.

The kitchen would be interesting to every practical housewife, for it incorporates not only the principles of hygiene and sanitation, but also most of the labor-saving devices so dear to the average woman. There is, for instance, an electric dishwasher, a vegetable-washer, a water filter, a grinder for grains or coffees, if one wishes, heaps of closet space, a gas incinerator and similar conveniences.

From the photographs of the exterior of the residence you can see the quantity of glass which makes the house really an outdoors home whenever so desired.

This home, in a sense, is being built mainly for the little ones. It is really a social school in which they will learn their life habits. Their customs will be molded and shaped therein.

With this in view, it has many of the features which schools should have, but most of them do not. There are, for instance, ample playground facilities with playground equipment to be added. There is a wading pond, where the boys can sail their boats and grow their fish.

An out-of-doors, yet inclosed also a schoolroom proper with provision their carpenter work, clay modeling other hand tools.

There are facilities for swimm basketball, handball and, in fact, other provision which can be devised is a reasonably small area of groun

Yet most of these are available to average small home—the cottage of a est means.

The entire home should be consider from a social sense rather than fro restricted private family residence place where friends and kin can ga —where children of the neighbor will prolong their stay voluntarily.

The pictures will show some of t best can be seen on the residence. These are some of the primary ob tives in opening this home for p inspection. The thought and care

Photograph by Willard D. Morgan, architect; Richard D. Neutra

Side view of home and garage.

chins," "rupture," "prostrate troubles," "constipation" and "pelvic troubles: men and women,"[3] as evidence of to the increasing preoccupation of Americans with the physical appearance and performance of their bodies.

Lovell saw in modern architecture a model for health, a mechanism for reconstructing the human: "When we learn to build our bodies with the same careful precision and the same scientific accuracy with which the modern builder constructs his houses."[4] Neutra, on the other hand, saw architecture as a "branch of preventive medicine." Influenced by Lovell's drug-less theories of health, he 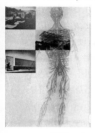 was proud of resisting the "drugs of ornamentation" in the design of the house, avoiding the "corpulent excesses of ornament and curvature."[5] Neutra had his own theories on the relationship between health and architecture, and wrote extensively about it. In *Survival through Design*← (1954), with all the nerves of the body on the back cover, he argues that the very survival of the human species depends on having designers focus on "physiological space." Design operates for Neutra at the intersection of biology and psychology as a therapeutic defense against the "disastrous effects" of all the accumulated conditions of modern life.

Neutra thought his buildings could not just improve the health but also the sex life of the inhabitants. The desire for self-improvement in every aspect of one's life resonated with Californians who had become increasingly concerned with their bodies' appearance and performance. Exercise, bodybuilding, dieting, therapy, surgery, and cosmetics became a major part of a continuous self-construction.[6] Already by midcentury, the preoccupation had extended to mental health. Neutra thought of the architect as a kind of shrink and among the functions of the house was to provide psychological well-being. Many clients of Neutra talked to him about their "nervous" problems, their marital problems, their fertility problems. In fact, his theory of architecture was a theory about the nerves, the intersection of body and brain.

A symptomatic figure was Wilhelm Reich, a protégé of Freud who deviated from his theories, was expelled from  psychoanalytic circles, and settled in America in 1939. He was the inventor of the *orgone energy accumulator*←, popularized as an "orgasm machine" in films like Woody Allen's *Sleeper* (1973) and Roger Vadim's *Barbarella* (1968). Several clients of Neutra were followers of Reich, especially Josephine and Robert Chuey, who commissioned a house by him that became a salon for orgone users and early experiments with LSD.[7]

Reich thought the libido was affected by physical space and, unlike Freud, who saw sexual dysfunction as a symptom of neurosis, Reich thought it was the cause of the neurosis and sought to alleviate it with "orgone," a previously unaccounted form of energy. His "orgone energy accumulator" was a primitive box the size of a telephone booth made of multiple layers (up to 20) of organic and nonorganic materials that was supposed to accumulate the energy and transmit it to the body inside it. Reich wrote about the need for regular, daily sessions in the machine and claimed it could cure anything from headaches to chronic fatigue, arthritis, heart disease, cancer, brain tumors, and impotence. The orgone accumulator became best known as a machine to increase sexual performance, or what Reich called "orgastic potency," a complete release of energy that could be measured as an electrical discharge. Several clients of Neutra had accumulators in their houses. More important, Neutra thought of the house itself as a kind of orgone accumulator, a machine not just for health but also for desire. Or rather desire as health.

Another émigré from Vienna, Frederick Kiesler, also saw as the primary responsibility of design "to satisfy the psyche of the dweller."[8] In his 1949 essay "Pseudo-Functionalism in Modern Architecture," he writes "the house is a human body, a living organism with the reactivity of a full-blooded creature," with organs (the stairs are the feet, the ventilation system the nose, and so on), a nervous system, and a digestive system that can "suffer from constipation."[9] More than that, he insists, the house, like man, lives "in emotions and dreams through the medium of his physique." The psyche cannot be separated from the body. Indeed, the house is the product of "the erotic and creative instinct," and its experience is erotic. For Kiesler, modern architecture was filled with repressions that needed to be unblocked in the name of pleasure.

In 1947 Kiesler had generated the first version of his Endless house. The house was not just one project among others. It was his whole life, his philosophy and even his body. He built it from the inside, literally, and saw himself being swallowed by it. The house was like a stomach, full of folds, absorbing juices and nutrients. The occupant becomes a kind of food. In an extraordinary confusion of his own body with architecture he describes modern architecture as architecture on a diet in the aftermath of World War I:

We had nothing to eat. I recall very well my own situation: after the war I lived on the dole for many years; I got about seven Kronen a week, which would be the equivalent of seven dollars per week now. But one could live on that monastically; I had rice, chiefly, and mushrooms. . . . I remember only too well the mushrooms, which I dried and reheated again just as I did with tea leaves. As in our living habits, we started to clean off everything that was surplus in design – ornamentation, certain luxurious materials, moldings, this and that. Everything became, over the years, simpler, cleaner, whiter, and . . . you know, what we call functionalism was on its natural way. So functionalism was really a reaction to the overstuffing of the Victorian age. Architecture had to be put on a diet. And the rectangular style did it. Now the period of diet is over and we can eat normally again. However, that does not mean that we should overeat, stuff ourselves with whipped cream, ice cream – or with architecture either.[10]

Just as Le Corbusier's ideas about health and architecture started with obsessions with his own body, Kiesler's physical condition organized his theories and designs. He could not separate himself from his architecture, could not be

separated from his shell. Symptomatically, *he always had his own body photographed inside the body of the building*←. With his fragile frame inside the egg-shaped house, it is as if it had become his surrogate body. He replaced the

heroic, athletic, muscular body of modern architecture with a frail body in need of protection by architecture. Architecture becomes an infinite, uterine cave, nurturing a kind of translucent body.

The polemical sensuality of his designs extends the nerves from the psyche through the tactile to the cosmic. In a series of sketches Kiesler makes this point. In one, the *interaction of the nervous system with a chair* becomes part of a multisensual engagement with the world. In another, the chair becomes part of an interior and the human is described as *"a terrestrial spectra,"* the environment as a "stellar spectra (with the objects taking the place of stars)." Space for Kiesler is always outer space and deep inner space. It is not by chance that his memoirs are entitled *Inside the Endless House*. Psyche, sexuality, the body, and architecture are inseparable.

Dissidents like Kiesler expose that modern design is an always failed attempt to repress its own sensuality. It is full of secrets, obsessions, and forbidden pleasures hidden just behind its attempts to project the image of a new normality.

Humans don't accept death. We resist it. We fight it. We spend enormous amount of energy and resources to delay it, to prolong life even under unbearable, "inhuman," conditions, and when it arrives, we honor it, we celebrate it. And again a huge amount of resources are deployed. Design is involved in every step, from the multiple elaborate inventions that have "saved" billions of lives to the myriad of rituals that every culture has developed to deal with death. One of the unique symptoms of the human species is the design of death. We are the species that buries its dead, and archaeological traces of burial sites are treated as crucial evidence of humanity. Even more than 100,000 years ago in the Middle East, nomadic hunter-gathers design burials and place designed objects on or beside the bodies. In the earliest permanent settlements, such as 10,500-year-old Boncuklu, in Turkey, bodies were buried under the floor of the oval mud-brick houses with stone tools and pieces of red ochre placed beside them. A thousand years later, in the earliest protocities like Çatalhöyük, up to thirty bodies were buried beneath the floor of each rectangular house as an integral part of the architecture. Not by chance did Adolf Loos use the burial mound as the primal sign of architecture in 1910. The design of death constantly evolves. Today there is a new emphasis on ecology, the carbon footprint of cremation, the lack of space for the dead in cities and even in the countryside. Designers have developed suits that turn corpses into mushrooms and stainless steel machines that chemically liquefy bodies. But the human is also unique in the design of life – the crafting of new forms of mechanical, electronic, and biological life. The ancient search for a thinking machine that would be indistinguishable from a human is nearing its goal. Whole new forms of life are genetically engineered in laboratories. Designing for life and death has been replaced by designing life itself.

"Mickey Mouse proves that a creature can still survive even when it has thrown off all resemblance to a human being. He disrupts the entire hierarchy of all creatures that is supposed to culminate in mankind. … the explanation for the huge popularity of these films is not mechanization, their form; nor is it a misunderstanding. It is simply the fact that the public recognizes its own life in them."

–Walter Benjamin

Frederick Kiesler, Endless House

12

DESIGN AS PERVERSION

Modern design was never straightforward. Despite the surface rhetoric of rationality, clarity, and efficiency, modern designers engaged with everything that escapes rationality: sexuality, violence, exoteric philosophies, occultism, disease, the psyche, pharmacology, extraterrestrial life, chance, the primitive, the animal, the fetish, etc.

Perversion comes from the Latin *pervertere*, "to turn away," that is, turning away from normality. There is a relationship between the personal, often extreme, pathologies of modern architects and their call for a new normal – a tension within which new concepts of the human emerge. But design perversions are not simply about the all-too-human pathologies of designers. It is about the construction of the human by modern design.

Le Corbusier, the single most influential architect of the twentieth century, was deeply into the occult, esoteric philosophies, sexual complexities, obsessed with the toilet, with disease, nudism, bodybuilding, the animal, and the other. For less well known figures like *Carlo Mollino*←, architecture and design are literally a product of perversion, so much so he is not easily placed in any traditional account of modern architecture. Historians don't know how to position him. So if we take these two extremes, Le Corbusier as a seemingly straight architect who is secretly twisted and Mollino as a seemingly twisted architect who is secretly at the center of modern architecture, the question is whether so-called perversions are twists of modern design or its very engine.

FETISHISM

The exhibition *Are Clothes Modern?* by Viennese émigré architect and designer Bernard Rudofsky opened at MoMA in 1944. It was meant to be a critique of MoMA's understanding of what modern design was. In Rudofsky's view the In-

ternational Style exhibition of 1932 had repressed everything that was interesting in modern architecture and design: the "primitive," the psychological, sensuality and the erotic.[1] A panel at the entry to the exhibition read: "Warning! This is NOT a fashion or dress reform show! ... It shows the maze of the irrational and accidental clothing habits from which it is time to escape." Rudofsky went on to quote Balzac: "Nothing resembles Man less than a Man," adding "Man has always been bored with his anatomy. He considers it only a point of departure for his creations."[2]

The exhibition challenged orthodox thinking about modernity by looking at the distorted bodies that correspond to the "personal torture devices" that are part of everyday clothing. Rudofsky developed a catalog of abnormal bodies lurking within presumably normal clothing. Specially sculpted figures and drawings showed the body as it would look like if it fitted the clothes it wears. Plaster figures designed by Rudofsky and modeled by sculptor Costantino Nivola showed a woman's body as if would be were it to fit the clothes of four fashion periods. *A tennis outfit of 1886* was shown next to a drawing by Rudofsky of the body implied by it. The literal torture of binding the feet of young Chinese girls, he claimed, was acted out daily on the streets in the West. He shows that the foot that corresponds to a "stylish" shoe in an advertisement of the 1920s, and still popular, is as deformed as a Chinese lily foot. Men's shoes were not much better. Rudofsky even argued that the torture of the feet by the seemingly straightforward western *Oxford shoes* would lead to new feet with the big toe in the middle. In fact, Rudofsky

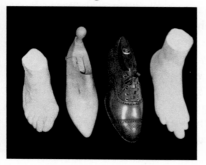

may have been onto something. The Oxford shoe, invented in the nineteenth century and popular then with university students, was cut smaller than the foot, unlike earlier shoes, in order to give men a mincing step. For Rudofsky, design was literally redesigning the body. In "Sartoriasis, or the Enjoyment of Discomfort," he speaks about the "masochistic" pleasure of these fetishistic practices.

Rudofsky countered the masochism of design with a more natural clothing and footwear. He was a practicing nudist who, in response to questions by the press, had to reassure his audience that his habit was "entirely private."[3] Like his Austrian colleagues in California, he was inspired by the ideas of the *Lebensreform* with its embrace of a return to nature, vegetarian diet, natural cures, nudism and loose robes.

Are Clothes Modern? aimed to show the similarities between design in "primitive" and modern cultures by juxtaposing ethnographic artifacts with objects of industrial design to reveal in Rudofsky's word, their "affinities." Along the corridors leading into the exhibition were representations of the human form from cave drawings through Renaissance engravings to modern fashion pictures. Rudofsky wrote in the catalog: "The civilized individual is not less a fetish worshipper than the savage."[4] He insisted that every one, man or woman, was a fetishist who did not think of it as a "pathological symptom."[5]

Rudofsky ended up designing a kind of counterfashion. Clothes and footwear that supposedly liberate the body were presented in the exhibition, like his famous Bernardo sandals, which went into production shortly after and are still available today. They were very popular in the 1950s and 60s. Jackie Kennedy was said to own sixteen pairs in different colors of the same model. And yet Rudofsky clearly enjoys the pornography of the deformed body with a particular obsession on the feet. His fetish is equally intense with the twisted foot as with the supposedly liberated one.

BONDAGE
In 1976–77, Bernard Tschumi produced a series of polemical *"Advertisements for Architecture↗,"* each as a kind of visual manifesto. They were first published accompanying his own articles in architecture and art journals such as *Oppositions*, *Architectural Design*, *Space Design*, and *Studio International* and exhibited as posters in galleries like PS1 and Artists Space. Eventually they were made into a series of postcards and sold widely.

In a parody of commercial advertising, each advertisement is a striking, sometimes shocking, image accompanied by a

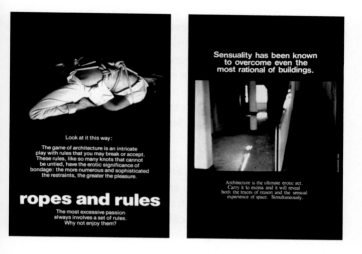

slogan. Each is transgressive. All the conventions of good design go out the window. Literally. An image of somebody thrown out of a high window goes with the slogan: "To really appreciate architecture you may even need to commit a murder." Another shows an image of a seminude person

completely tied up with thick, intricately knotted ropes. The text suggests that architecture is a form of pleasurable bondage through the constraints of self-imposed rules: "The game of architecture is an intricate play with rules that you may break or accept. These rules, like so many knots that cannot be untied, have the erotic significance of bondage: the more numerous and sophisticated the restraints, the greater the pleasure." Another advertisement shows Villa Savoye, the canonic building of Le Corbusier, in a state of decay, and relishes its eroticism: "Sensuality has been known to overcome even the most rational of buildings: Architecture is the ultimate erotic art. Carry it to excess and it will reveal both the traces of reason and the sensual experience of space. Simultaneously."

The advertisements coincide with a set of interrelated essays on the relationship between architecture and transgression, eroticism, violence, pleasure, and limits, deeply influenced by Georges Bataille, Roland Barthes, Antonin Artaud, and Philippe Sollers, as is polemically clear in Tschumi's titles: "Architecture and Transgression" (1975), "The Pleasure of Architecture" (1977), "Architecture and Limits" (1980), "Violence of Architecture" (1981). Tschumi challenges designers to consider the possibility that there is no such a thing as an innocent design. The most basic definition and occupation of space has illicit resonances.

> Any relationship between a building and its users is one of violence, for any use means the intrusion of a human body into a given space, the intrusion of one order into another. . . . The love of violence, after all, is an ancient pleasure. Why has architectural theory regularly refused to acknowledge such pleasures and always claimed (at least officially) that architecture should be pleasing to the eye, as well as comfortable to the body? . . . The pleasure of violence can be experienced in every other human activity.[6]

The much-advertised morality of design turns out to be a dissimulating mask. The controlled lines of design are exactly that: control, authority, constraint, repression and pleasure.

In 1949 Le Corbusier built a small wooden cabin (the Cabanon) for himself overlooking the beach at Cap Martin, in the south of France, where he would swim every day and where he eventually died, while swimming, in August 1965.

The cabin was built at the very limits of the adjacent property, right behind E.1027, the remarkable house designed and built by Eileen Gray between 1926 and 1929 for herself and Jean Badovici, editor of the French architectural journal *L'Architecture vivante*. Le Corbusier occupied and controlled the site of E.1027 by overlooking it, the cabin being little more than an observation platform, a sort of "*watchdog house↑*," as Gray herself put it.[7]

The word *obsession* is inadequate to describe *Le Corbusier←*'s relationship to this house and to Eileen Gray herself. Le Corbusier systematically colonized E.1027, covering it with murals without permission, allowing himself to be credited for the house and even organizing to own it by proxy after the death of Badovici. All of the psychosexual intensity of Le Corbusier's relentless fascination with the other, cultivated through his encounter with the "women of Algiers," is exacerbated here in the encounter with a lesbian architect and designer.

His study for the murals in E.1027 began with his drawing of Algerian women in the spring of 1931. He said that he had been "profoundly seduced by a type of woman particularly well built," of which he made many nude studies.[8] He also acquired a big collection of colored postcards depicting naked women surrounded by accoutrements from the Oriental bazaar. Le Corbusier filled three notebooks of sketches of nude women in Algiers that he later claimed were stolen from his Paris atelier. But Ozenfant denies it, saying that Le Corbusier himself either destroyed or hid them, considering them a "secret d'atelier."[9] The Algerian *sketches and postcards*↑ are an ordinary instance of the ingrained fetishistic appropriation of women, of the East, of "the other." Yet Le Corbusier turned this material into endless studies for a mural that preoccupied him for the rest of his life.

From the months immediately following his return from Algiers, Le Corbusier made hundreds of sketches on yellow tracing paper by laying it over the original sketches and redrawing the contours of the figures. That the drawing and redrawing of these images became a lifetime obsession already indicates that something was at stake. This became even more obvious when in 1963–64, shortly before his death, Le Corbusier, unhappy with the visible aging of the yellow tracing paper, copied a selection of twenty-six drawings onto transparent paper and, symptomatically for someone who kept everything, burned the rest.

But the process of drawing and redrawing the women of the Casbah reached its most intense, if not hysterical, moment when Le Corbusier's studies found their way into a set of eight murals he completed in 1938 in E.1027, having borrowed the house for a spring vacation. Le Corbusier referred to one of the murals as *Graffite à Cap Martin* and other times he labeled it *Three Women*↑.[10] Le Corbusier "explained to his friends that 'Badou' [Badovici] was depicted on the right, his friend Eileen Gray on the left; the outline of the head and the hairpiece of the sitting figure in the middle, he claimed, was 'the desired child, which was never born.'"[11]

Le Corbusier's violation of Gray's house and identity is consistent with his fetishization of Algerian women. More important, this obsession seem to have structured his entire life. Can this be put to one side as the private life of a designer? Or is it the very engine of design?

EROTICA
And what to make of *Mollino*←, architect, interior designer, furniture maker, engineer, photographer, fashion designer, set designer, car designer, patent inventor, novelist, stunt pilot, champion skier, racing car driver, professor of architecture, author? Marginalized in architectural history as

"enigmatic," "nonconformist," "elusive," "individualistic," "lone wolf," "troublesome," "unique case," "marginal," "special," "eccentric," "turbulent," "holy madman," "prima donna," "diabolic," "occult worshiper," "unconventional at all costs," "dissolute," "erotomaniac," "kinky," and "dangerous," Mollino can never be pinned down and there is an irreducible sense of the illicit.

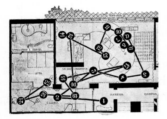

In 1936 Carlo Mollino made an apartment for himself, *Casa Miller*← in Torino, but he never actually lived there. The space was designed to house his fantasies. He used it to photograph women friends and clients. It was a stage set for erotic fantasies, with every detail organized to facilitate the best camera angles.

In 1960, he went much further, designing a secret apartment that not even his closest friends knew about, Casa Mollino in Via Napione, Turin. Unlike in the Casa Miller, the women he photographed were women he had never seen before and he would never see again. He would cruise the streets and clubs of Turin and identify women that his driver would come to later and offer a huge amount of money to meet Mollino in his apartment. But Mollino never had sex with any of them. They would be dressed in outfits designed by Mollino, including the shoes, the veils, the underwear, etc. Mollino took thousands of *Polaroid images* ⤾ for a secret album. The fantasy was that these women would accompany him in the afterlife. The whole apartment was designed as a tomb, with all the paraphernalia of safe passage to the afterlife. He slept in a bed designed as a boat to cross the last river, surrounded by butterflies, the icon of reincarnation.

SCATOLOGY

The entire history of modern design could be written from the point of view of the toilet. Modern architects turned private bathrooms into public spaces and in so doing sexualized architecture. From Adolf Loos and his poetry on American plumbing to Le Corbusier, who celebrated sanitary fixtures and positioned them prominently on view in the spaces of his houses, to Paul Rudolph's town house in Manhattan, where the entrance lobby provides a view up through the bottom of the glass bathtub above, modern architecture challenged traditional morality.

Loos's writings are full of scatological references. In his magazine *Das Andere: Journal for the Introduction of Western Culture in Austria* (1902–3), he compares Austria to America in terms of the use of toilet paper (absent in the former and ubiquitous in the latter). And in his essay

AUTRES ICONES
LES MUSÉES

Il y a les bons musées, puis les mauvais. Puis ceux qui ont
pêle-mêle du bon et du mauvais. Mais le musée est une entité
consacrée qui circonvient le jugement.

"The Plumbers" (1898) he wrote that "the only works of art America has given are her plumbing and her bridges,"[12] anticipating by almost two decades Marcel Duchamp, who in response to the rejection of his *Fountain* by the Salon of the Independents for being "plagiarism, a plain piece of plumbing" said, in the words of Beatrice Wood: "The only works of art America has given are her plumbing and her bridges."[13]

Le Corbusier thought the *bidet was worthy of a museum*↖. The first demand of his "Manuel de l'habitation" was for a bathroom that would take the place of the drawing room.[14] The bidet was a major polemical device, placed on view, challenging the prevailing codes of the day and arousing charges of immorality. In the Weissenhof Siedlung in Stuttgart (1927), where all the leading architects of the time presented their concept of domestic life, Le Corbusier was denounced for having the bidet in the middle of the open space, which is simultaneously bedroom and living space. Newspaper articles attacked Le Corbusier for an arrangement that, they claimed, would only make sense in a brothel. The press was also scandalized by the half-height wall screening the bathroom from the bedroom, imagining the smell and the sounds and arguing that the arrangement only made sense in a brothel or for those with "immoral habits."[15]

It was not the first time that Le Corbusier had used plumbing fixtures in a polemical way. In his own apartment in Paris, in Nungesser et Coli, Le Corbusier put the bidet *in the middle of the space*↑, apparently embarrassing even his wife, Yvonne, who used to cover it with a tea towel when they had visitors. Le Corbusier considered the toilet "one of the most beautiful objects industry has produced" and in his Cabanon, he left the toilet open to the space. In Villa Savoye, his most famous house, the first thing you see when you enter is a plumbing fixture, a white sink positioned at the beginning of the white promenade like a work of art in a museum. And the most elaborate space in the house is the bathroom, with its sunken bathtub and built-in chaise longue in blue tiles like a sensuous body in the space, or the space itself becoming a sensual body. The bathroom is not really a room. It is open to the rest of the house thereby sexualizing the whole internal landscape.

Buckminster Fuller completed in 1938 the design for the Dymaxion bathroom, a compact, self-sufficient instrument for dealing with all of the body's most intimate needs. It was a flying capsule, a miniature autonomous architecture based on Fuller's intense obsession with hygiene and daily rituals of internal and external cleansing.

The toilet literally took off in the 1960s. Fuller expanded the concept of the toilet into that of a spaceship. For him, all houses were spaceships and all spaceships were houses. Mankind was always in outer space and was destined to return one day to whatever planet it had already come from by radio beam. Body, brain, and building were just bundles of frequencies. Toilet and telepathy were inseparable.

Meanwhile, Le Corbusier was getting more and more into the toilet. From 1957 to 1959, he came up with a number of toilet designs for the Pozzi Company. He *studied shitting*← in great detail, obsessed with all the positions customary in different cultures, making a series of drawings. He had already designed, with Charlotte Perriand, a prefabricated sanitary cabin for public use for an international exhibition in Paris in 1937 where the toilet can be used crouching (Turkish style) or sitting down and where the bidet can be flipped over the toilet.

PEDOPHILIA

When Loos himself arrived in Paris in 1926, he was on the run, accused of pederasty in Vienna, a fact carefully concealed until recently in the scholarship on Loos. The moralizing tone of "Ornament and Crime" (1908),

arguably the single most influential essay of the twentieth century, which associates ornament with sexual degeneracy, is simply absorbed by the field without reflection. Likewise, the deep sensuality and polemical eroticism of his buildings is never seen to be in conflict with his essay. So deep is the repression of the field of architecture that everybody acts as if Loos's architecture is not ornamented. In the end, neither the essay not the buildings are read. The furry bedroom for his first teenage bride and the voyeuristic swimming pool he provides for Josephine Baker are treated as aberrations of an otherwise proper architect.

For all the advertised morality of design, those who design and those who use the designs do so in deeply charged ways, taking pleasure in ways that the official discourse cannot acknowledge, yet may form the very engine of design. Design might always be driven by desire. Design might always be a crime. The human is never simple or straightforward.

Elsie Altmann, second wife of Adolf Loos, ca. 1916

Machines are increasingly asking us to demonstrate that we are human. The CAPTCHA (Completely Automated Public Turing Test to Tell Computers and Humans Apart), invented in 2003, presents online users with a simple puzzle that machine intelligence was unable to do, like reading the letters of a warped word. When artificial intelligence was able to solve such puzzles in 2014, a new system was introduced. It asks you to confirm a single remarkable statement: "I am not a robot." Your answer is not the point. The self-adjusting program determines if you are human by monitoring how you interact with the content on the page before and after you click. Everyday life echoes the existential dilemma posed in countless books, movies, and TV series where all-too-human machines cannot be distinguished from humans behaving like robots. The constant labor of proving that you are yourself, with passwords and biometrics offering a thin and fragile defense against the traumatic threat of identity theft, gives way to the labor of proving that you are not yet a machine.

"If it works,
it's obsolete."

–Marshall McLuhan

Bedroom for Lina Loos, Adolf Loos, 1903

13

DESIGNING
A GHOST

Every designer gives birth to a strange
life-form, a portable inanimate human that
joins the ranks of a new species that is
dispersed across the landscape of design.

Almost every design studio keeps one of the manuals of
standardized "human" dimensions, like those of Ernst
Neufert and Henry Dreyfuss, close at hand. Yet the
crisply silhouetted figures that organize those manuals
rarely appear in the drawings of designers. The generic
humans that so effortlessly organize any space, occupy any
furniture, perform any activity, and cross any national or
cultural border in the pages of the manuals are only used
as a source of reliable measures for furniture, equipment,
and spaces. The received "normal" is quickly discarded
and replaced by an equally schematic "scale figure" of
the designer's own making – a redesigned human. This
figure can be drawn very quickly, usually in a single line,
whether in a squiggle or a sharp geometric shape. It is
the most minimal gesture to represent the human. Each
designer invents their own unique avatar that paradoxically
represents all possible users of the design. It somehow
already embodies the philosophy of the designer and
appears in project after project as a kind of signature,
having typically been developed early in the designer's
career and faithfully repeated with minor variations.

The scale figure is typically neither old nor young and has no mouth, eyes, or limbs, let alone tools. It usually just floats there, not having the feet to really stand. Occasionally it is seated on a piece of furniture sympathetically offered to it but is rarely active, or even sleeping. It is just suspended in the space of design, motionless. It is devoid of internal physiology, hair, gender, race, senses, emotions, or opinions. It usually appears alone or in different parts of the same design, as when a figure appears on the ground floor and an uncannily identical figure appears on the terrace and again inside an office. When more than one appear in the same space, they do not interact with each other, even when side by side. If you met a group of scale figures at a party they could not talk, eat, drink, or move – no matter how exciting it might be for them to finally be out of their usual interior and with others for the first time. They represent us, or the possibility of us, but what are they thinking?

The scale figure is a person without qualities, yet shaped, and shaped differently by each designer as either the starting point of design, the needy figure to be equipped and sheltered, or the desired outcome of design.

This indeterminate figure is a thoroughly twentieth-century creature directly associated with the arrival of modern architecture in the early 1920s. It would appear very strange if drawn into a nineteenth-century streetscape or interior – out of place and out of time, an alien. Its quasi humanity is somehow dependent on an environment of modern design. Which is not to say that it is simply at home in modern design either. On the contrary, it is modern precisely in the way that it floats in the newly designed world without fully engaging it, like a ghost haunting modern design.

In a sense, these barely defined figures affirm that the human is a question mark, a work in progress, with design seen as a crucial part of that progress. The development of a design project is often paralleled by the development of the figure, which becomes ever more detailed and active as the design moves from diagrammatic sketches toward final renderings. The minimal avatar in the early drawings turns into a carefully rendered figure or appropriated photograph at the end. Design appears to turn the protohuman into a human. Design grows humans. As the project gains detail, the floating in vitro figure becomes actively engaged as its feet now touch the floor, its arms rest on the furniture, its eyes see the environment for the first time, and its face becomes expressive; it is joined by other humans and they interact. It is as if one of the effects of design is social life itself in addition to physiological sensations, emotions, mentality, and activity. There is nothing innocent in the figures haunting design drawings.

If design is always the design of the human, this schematic species is a crucial symptom. They are the first occupants of modern design that inhabit it even before the design is finished, the protohumans that test-drive the prototypes of modern design, as if to see if they will become human. Or is it that the ghost is a temporary substitute for the human that will itself be substituted by the design? Or even that it is exactly that, a ghost, the fragile trace of a human already departed, more posthuman than protohuman?

Modern design was dedicated to the emergence of a new human with its own speed, physiology, and nervous system for whom neoclassical architecture was no longer appropriate, a figure that was as carefully designed as the equipment it would use and the buildings it would occupy. But this organism was incubated in the margins of the drawings of designers, not at the center. It emerged as a kind of effect of the designs being presented, a flickering figure, not always there, not very there even when there, and never the same. This is not a heroic creature at ease with its own modernity. On the contrary, it was severely traumatized. It is not by chance it first appeared after the unambiguous distress of World War I. The difference in the way the human was rendered before and after the extended destruction of people and places is palpable.

Proto-modern designers at the turn of the twentieth century like Otto Wagner, Frank Lloyd Wright, Hendrik Petrus Berlage, and Peter Behrens presented their designs as a kind of interface between human and machine. They engaged the increasingly mechanized world and the new forms of life that it supported but also tried to protect the rapidly evolving human. Design was a form of defense, and the body was typically wrapped in clothing that matched the buildings, furnishings, and objects. Renderings featured highly detailed figures whose clothing and activities harmonized with the designed spaces and objects, with the human seemingly modernizing itself in synchrony with the designs around it.

Otto Wagner, the first to publish a manifesto on "Modern Architecture" (1896), spoke of the new needs of "modern man" in terms of "new human tasks and viewpoints" and of "human clothing" as the original beginning of art in industry. He played a major role in the industrial transformation of Vienna, acting as one of the most

ZINSHAUS 'WIEN 'VI 'NEUSTIFTG '40'

OBERBAURAT 'OTTO 'WAGNER

influential agents of modernization but also providing design as a prophylactic – protecting the concept of the human even as that concept evolved dramatically. His thirty-six train stations for the new transit network softened the abrupt transition from the streets down to the tracks that had rapidly cut their way into the heart of the city with their new speed, rhythm, and sounds. The stations were not just inserted into the gap between human and machine. They are themselves a form of clothing to be worn by both people and trains. Wagner's drawings of the new stations, bridges, buildings, and neighborhoods of the modernizing city are populated with an astonishing array of highly detailed children running, women talking, men with walking sticks, and the elderly. They are all actively engaging in metropolitan life in carefully designed outfits, whether *street cleaning* or promenading. The new urban creature is shown happily occupying its modernized habitat. Wagner deployed the standard *école des beaux-arts* technique of placing human figures in the final renderings, but did so to push neoclassical architecture aside. The clothing he drew was modernized to match the redesigned city. More precisely, modern design itself was presented as dress reform, with the façades appearing as newly thin garments.

As architecture and industrial design were increasingly stripped down to a smooth shell by the 1920s, so too was the figure and its clothing. The human had long been enveloped by galaxies of diagnostic instruments and associated sciences that treated the body as a machine, turned into a silhouette without gender, personal, social, or political identity to be analyzed only in terms of work by relentlessly studying the physiological rhythms and flows of energy in its nerves and muscles. The smooth outline of the industrialized body and its movements became blurred with the smooth outlines of the machines, obliging designers to continually restate their loyalty to the human specificity that was seemingly being erased.

Walter Gropius, for example, orchestrated a sustained attempt to design the "new human" as director of the Bauhaus, the school that did the most to consolidate the modern concept of industrial design and is still emblematic of the concept of design today. The founding manifesto of the Bauhaus in 1919 centered its experimental work on the damaged, traumatized, and obsolete human figure immediately after the war: "The old forms are in ruins, the benumbed world is shaken up, the old human spirit is invalidated and in flux toward a new form."[1] Having been seriously wounded in 1918, Gropius repeatedly tried to counter any perception that the school was abandoning the human in favor of the standardizing logic of the machine. His 1925 *New Architecture and the Bauhaus*, for example, insisted that his thinking, like that of most fellow architects, was galvanized by the "violent interruption" of the war that called for "an intellectual change of front."[2] The dehumanizing effects of unrestrained mechanization are condemned: "Were mechanization an end in itself it would be an unmitigated calamity . . . stunting men and women into sub-human, robot-like automatons."[3] His *Internationale Architektur* survey of the same year, based on the exhibition he had curated two years before at the Bauhaus, identified "humanity" (*Menschheit*) as the most important guiding principle.[4] Yet the drawings and photographs presented in the survey are almost completely devoid of human figures. Page after page of buildings sit on empty streets with only the occasional car going by, as if all the images combine to form a single polemical image of an uninhabited landscape of modern architecture spreading itself across the world.

The new human does lurk in the middle of the survey in the rendering of *Gropius↓* and Adolf Meyer's own entry to the Chicago Tribune Tower competition of 1922. A single tiny figure stands on the street corner below the corner of the building. It is an abstract outline with distinct legs but no arms, eyes, ears, or hair. It is boxy, almost like a building element, and has the same shading as the building that it casts a strong shadow onto. It could be masculine, yet this same armless figure is very carefully drawn on the elevation drawing in such a way that it could be wearing either a suit or a dress – again standing at the corner

of the building and the corner of the drawing. This anonymous, androgynous, ageless metropolitan creature is modern precisely in being somehow detached from the world that it is either entering or emerging from. More precisely, it hovers at the threshold of modern design without any clue as to whether it is entering or leaving, profoundly alone, like the building itself which has no neighbors in the image.

Not by chance does one of the most famous photographs of Gropius show him in his crisp suit and bow tie standing next to this rendering of the skyscraper, his body having more or less the same size as the building it overlaps, as if humanizing it. The larger-than-life figure of the designer even stands facing us at the same angle as his tiny protohuman figure.

Similar schematic humans appear in Mart Stam's 1922 competition drawing for the design of a stock exchange in Konigsberg that Gropius had exhibited in 1923 and was published in Adolf Behne's 1926 *Der moderne Zweckbau* (The Modern Functional Building).[5] Two *see-through figures*→ walk by on the street corner, ghosts that are defined only by an outline, presumably unable to see the building they are passing. They are descendants of the see-through

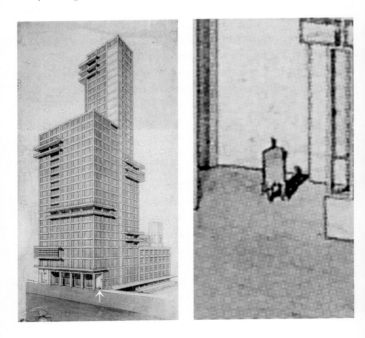

figures that pass in front of Tony Garnier's Heliotherapy
Pavilion in his *Cité Industrielle* project (1905), an image
that is symptomatically published in both the books of
Gropius and Behne. Garnier's humans still have faces and
detail of their modern clothing as distinct from their body,
and accessories like umbrellas and walking sticks, as do
Gropius's up until the war, like the two women floating
in front of the rendering of his model office and factory
for the 1914 Deutscher Werkbund exhibition in Cologne
that are starting to have a distinct drawn outline but still
have faces and very precise hand gestures, feet, hats, and
dresses. But Stam's faceless, armless, genderless ghosts are
constructed out of a single line. A new human has been
invented as a kind of guest from the future. Sometimes it's
only a blackened silhouette, as with one of the three tiny
figures dwarfed by the elevation of Mies van der Rohe's
Glass Skyscraper Project (1922) or the two little isolated
figures on opposite street corners below Lissitsky and
Stam's Horizontal Skyscraper (1924) that are completely
detached from the building and from the even more

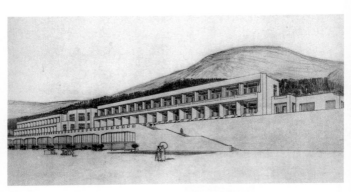

Tony Garnier, Heliotherapy Pavilion, *Une Cité Industrielle*

shadowy solitary figure that can be seen behind the glass on
the top floor of one of the renderings. In image after image,
the modern subject stands in front of modern architecture as
if in front of an empty ship that has just arrived. Even when
positioned within the interior, it is somehow detached from
the ghostship, floating inside the floating design, its very
presence emphasizing the emptiness.

These ghosts are precisely not the clear-cut industrialized
figures of ergonomic calculation that will be fully integrated
into the modern environment. Rather, they lurk in the
vicinity of modern design. Once invented in the early
1920s, they haunt twentieth-century design in countless

sketches, diagrams, and
renderings. Designers like Gropius
immediately started to experiment
with different ways to render
these lonely figures and some,
like Mies van der Rohe, became
experts, using the blur of long
exposure photographs in collages,

shadowy charcoal smears and delicate pencil outlines —
even using statues seen through glass to produce the effect
in the built work.

Yet finally humans are not so present in the images of modern
design. Objects, systems, buildings, neighborhoods, rooms,
and circuits are only occasionally visited by the human. The
majority of books on design are devoid of the creatures
they are supposedly dedicated to. For all the lip service
paid to the human in design theory, it ultimately does not
play a major role in design discourse precisely because it is
seen to be represented and upgraded by design itself. The
human is but a ghost, a shadowy figure that does not have
to be there. At once protohuman and posthuman, it has
always yet to arrive or has just left.

Horizontal Skyscraper, Lissitsky and Stam

We are surrounded in the streets, in buildings, in planes, boats, trains, and toilets by generic avatars of the human. Cities are inhabited by thousands upon thousands of diagrammatic people that live, for example, inside traffic lights. We stand at a street corner and a pixelated silhouette constructed out of a cluster of little red lights stands opposite us, as if in a mirror. It disappears and is replaced by a green figure that appears to be walking. We cross the street, faithfully imitating the image of a human. Decisions about which toilet to use are based on whether one of these figures on the door appears to have a dress or not, as if these are the only two options. Another one earnestly drops something into a diagrammatic waste can, encouraging us to do the same. Those that do a forbidden activity are placed in a circle with a diagonal line crossing it out as a warning. But usually these humanoids use their circular heads to do the right thing, staying in the right lane, wearing the right safety hat and safety glasses. They are especially well behaved in emergencies – knowing how to use a fire extinguisher and where the exits and stairs are. They are posted in every space, like guards that never move from their position. But they earnestly walk, run, sit, and swim on the spot. They use wheelchairs, bicycles, horses, and skis. Some walk dogs. If gathered together, they would form a comprehensive portrait of human activity – but a less than human portrait since these figures never yell, cry, go to the toilet that they guard, or change their minds. We are supposed to identify with these model citizens, even to obey them. But none of us look like them or think like them.

"My dream is to have people working on useless projects. These have the germ of new concepts."

–Charles Eames

Mies van der Rohe, Glass Skyscraper

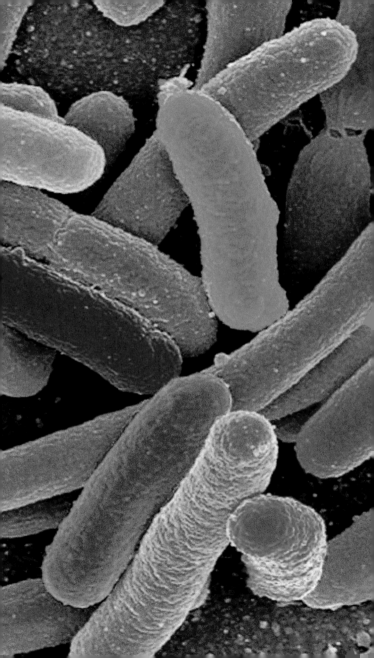

14

THE UNSTABLE BODY

The human is never simply human. Tens of thousands of different species are suspended within each human body and the body is itself suspended within a dense environment of countless species outside it. It is never clear where the human begins and ends.

The body is inhabited and constituted by thousands of microbes – many of which have existed for millions of years and have evolved in parallel with our species – upon which it depends for survival.[1] Only around 10 percent of "our" cells are human and only around 1 percent of the genetic material and even that 1 percent is mainly code from prior and parallel species. The human is a mobile cross-species collaboration and the collaboration is fluid, multiple, and ever-shifting. Each part of the interior and exterior of the body is inhabited by different sets of microbes. Each person has a different mix of microbes and the mix keeps changing during a lifetime. Childhood, pregnancy, illness, and old age initiate major shifts in the balance of organisms. Even going to the toilet changes the balance. The microbiome project that is trying to map this vast interspecies complex has completely changed the human self-image. Should human-centered design be centered on these microbes?

The human-specific parts of the human genome are very hard to find. Only 1 percent is different from that of a chimpanzee and just 10 percent from that of a cat. Scientists are trying to map the mutations in the genes that may have given the anatomically modern human – *Homo sapiens* – its decisive advantage over other all the other hominin species. The Neanderthal, its closest relative, shared 99.5 percent of the same genome but became extinct as the modern human flourished. The nature of this advantage is further complicated by the fact that 2 percent of today's non-African human genome comes from the interbreeding with the Neanderthal that happened in the Middle East around 100,000 years ago after *Homo sapiens* had migrated out of Africa, then again in Europe around 45,000 years ago. The genome of the human even includes sequences resulting from gene swaps with the microbes that inhabit the body, swaps that have played a key role in the evolution of the species.[2] The human is unique in its capacity to redesign things and itself, yet is completely suspended within a genetic matrix in intimate proximity to countless other species. Human specificity is elusive at best.

In reverse, each human body is highly unique within its own species, marked by idiosyncratic dimensions, fingerprints, ears, eyes, and DNA sequence. The human body is never singular or stable. On the contrary, it is defined by diversity, fluidity, and transformation. Yet this diversity is continuously subjected to multiple cultural disciplines that attempt to normalize bodies into stable codes of gender, sexuality, ethnicity, nationality, globality, prosperity, subservience, and speed – even to establish certain bodies as invisible or disposable, or simply not human. These codes are design codes, reinforced by self-fashioning protocols of makeup, shaving, haircuts, exercise, diet, fashion, adornment, posture, ways of moving, and so on. There are

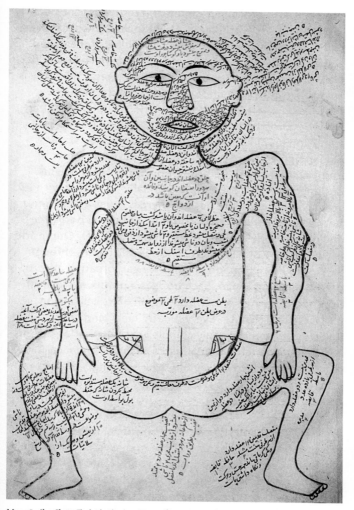

Mansūr ibn Ilyās *Tashrīh-i badan-i insān* (Anatomy of the Human Body), ca. 1390

different norms for repackaging and reshaping the body in the streets, in workplaces, social spaces, private spaces, and in social media. There is no such thing as the naked human body. The human becomes human in changing itself. Darwin said we even designed our nakedness. The body is an artifact, the product of protocols and technologies.

Design is prosthetic, producing new human bodies by transforming old ones. The image of a singular stable human figure served by design is a fantasy, an effect of design rather than its starting point. The body itself is designed. It is remade deeply and daily – starting with its very silhouette. Before design, there is never a clear line between the inside and outside of the human body, the end of one body and the beginning of another. Our inside is made of the outside that continuously passes through it. We are literally made of what we eat, breathe, absorb, digest, and synthesize. Each body is a porous system, all flow and exchange with three million of its cells being replaced each minute. Every breath, meal, and touch involves the unimaginably complex exchange of organisms and genetic material that triggers chains of chemical reactions and electrical signals. Our seemingly distinct form is like a mirage, a relatively slow-moving effect of countless exchanges.

This extreme fluidity between the inside and the outside of the body is the very basis of much non-Western medicine where it is understood as a matter of dynamic balance with the cosmos. With the invention of modern Western medicine through the rise of laboratory science, the body was treated as a closed system that can be reengineered, a construction site in which every element and process can be adjusted, magnified, suppressed, or replaced with different technologies. But no one is so simply or straightforwardly

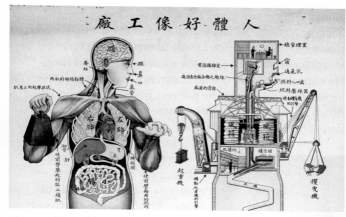

Chinese public health poster, ca. 1933

modern. Many different understandings of the body are usually maintained at the same time. People who see their body as an integral part of the cosmos, almost dissolving into the fabric of the world, might still treat their body with the latest technologies and chemicals. In reverse, those who usually think of their body as a sophisticated machine can still turn to non-Western medicine. In a sense, we all maintain a set of different bodies, and much of cultural life requires people to imagine a different body in different occasions, and none of these bodies is simple.

We routinely replace parts on the inside of our body, like fillings in a tooth, and supplementary attachments on the outside, like glasses. These replacements and adjustments are not experienced as changes. They are fully integrated into the idea of the "natural" body. There may be a temporary awareness of inhabiting a reconstructed body when a whole tooth is replaced with a metal implant or the glasses are made unnecessary by reshaping the eye with laser surgery, but this sense quickly passes. The very idea of adding new body parts and removing others has become routine. All the techniques of the artificial body that were once advanced medical experiments have steadily normalized. Even the doubling of the average life expectancy over the last century (with the greatest increases occurring in the poorest parts of the world, like Africa) is evidence of a whole new body. The human is simply not what it used to be.

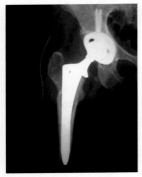

The interior of our bodies is increasingly filled with new mechanical parts. A galaxy of screws, plates, nails, wires, and stents in metal, ceramic, or plastic are added to support broken, weakened, or diseased body parts. Body parts themselves can be replaced, like *bones*←, joints, valves, tendons, veins, nerves, spinal discs, skull, ear, and nose – whether manufactured or transplanted from another part of the body or from another body. Hands, for example, are now replaced so often from human donors that both hands have to be replaced to make the news. Whole faces are being transplanted – complete with scalp, ears, ear

canals, bones from chin, cheeks, nose, eyelids, and the muscles that control blinking. Meanwhile, the kinds of tissue that can be transplanted keeps expanding (blood, skin, marrow, cornea, connective tissue, etc.), as does the number of organs (*heart*←, kidney, bladder, lungs, stomach, pancreas, intestine, thymus, ovary,

testes, penis, vagina, trachea, etc.) – whether taken from another human, from an animal, synthetic, 3D printed out of biomaterial, or even grown from the patient's own stem cells in laboratories.

External prosthetics keep expanding, from the traditional replacement of hands, arms, feet, and legs with metal, wooden, and plastic substitutes to electromechanical devices to neuroprosthetics that use the electrical signals in the nerves, or even brain waves to activate them. Since their ancient origins as techniques for addressing the effects of disease, war, and accidents, prosthetics can address a functional disability, make a body seem complete or more beautiful or enhance its performance. They repeat the movements and look of the body parts that they replace or add an entirely different set of movements, looks, or abilities that increase or accelerate the potential of the

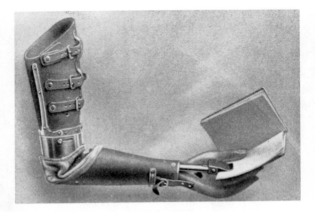

body. Prosthetics have an uncanny quality as they allow the human to feel human, yet don't seem to *need the body*↑, or have *surrogate parts of the body*↗ attached to them. Even more strangely, there is something human about them even before they are attached. The body is dramatically transformed, but the added element is fully integrated into the sense of self. Prosthetics are not so much attached as grafted into the body, an integration facilitated by the temperature, pressure, light, and sound sensors on the latest prosthetics that generate electrical impulses sent back into the nerves to give a sense of touch, feel, sight, and hearing.

Neuroprosthetics are increasingly integrated inside the

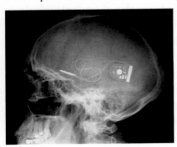

body. *Retinal implants*←, for example, have wires going from the inside of the eyeball to the brain. Cochlear implants likewise restore hearing. Neural stimulators attached to the spine control seizures or urination. Direct electrical

stimulation of areas of the brain controls epilepsy or enhances the ability to learn. Electrodes embedded in functioning muscles and wired to electrodes in paralyzed muscles allow stroke victims or paraplegics to stand, walk, or grasp. Intelligent exoskeletons enable the incapacitated to walk, with some guided by the electrical signals in the brain. These expensive high-technology procedures are paralleled by the 3D printing of low-cost open-source designs for prosthetic hands and legs that even include *control by nerves*↓. High-functioning inexpensive prosthetics, like the Jaipur foot developed in India, which have been fitted for free to more than 1.5 million people.

Reconstructive surgery becomes ever more sophisticated in making and disguising major changes to the body to address trauma, disease, birth defects, aesthetic preferences or gender reassignment. The body is systematically rebuilt and reshaped. The length of legs is adjusted. Breasts are enlarged or reduced. Intestines are shortened to reduce weight. Fat is sucked out. Plastic surgery is able to adjust or radically transform the shape, color, and texture of almost every dimension of the body. Plastic surgery in some parts of the world creates new kinds of urbanism. Entire neighborhoods, like Gangnam in Seoul, are devoted to all the phases of personal reconstruction, including special passport services to cater to the redesigned patient who is no longer recognizable at the border. The label "plastic surgery" was coined at the end of the eighteenth century and refers to a very long history of techniques to reconstruct the body in the face of war, accident, disease, perceived deformity, and ideals of physical beauty. Sophisticated Egyptian surgical techniques are recorded in 2000 BC and the *Sushruta Samhita* collection of medical texts from 600 BC includes the detailed description of techniques to rebuild a nose out of a cheek. Roman surgeons experimenting on injured gladiators developed techniques for reconstructing ears, lips, and noses in the first century BC. The surgeon Gaspare Tagliacozzi of Bologna published the first textbook in 1597. Modern plastic surgery – which was developed during World War I to deal with the unprecedented number of disfigurements,

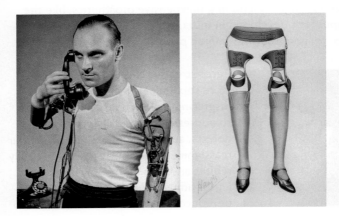

Portrait of Aimee Mullins by Howard Schatz, 2007

particularly of the face, and was accelerated by World War II and the Korean War – has now become part of everyday life. It is a design decision in an age in which bodies are more radically reconstructed than buildings.

Prosthetics, whose development was also accelerated to deal with the number of limbs lost on twentieth-century battlefields, are also evolving from life support for a damaged body to a strategic design decision. It becomes increasingly common to have several different artificial legs with different aesthetics and capacities. Choosing an appropriate leg is like choosing the right shoe.

The whole concept of life support has changed as technologies move from emergency rooms and operating theaters to domestic life. Much of the equipment of the hospital has migrated into the domestic environment. People routinely monitor an array of physiological indicators in their bodies with a level of precision and attention once associated with doctors, and self-medicate.

The body is just as dramatically redesigned with drugs. There is an extraordinary daily intake of a wide range of chemicals introduced into the body to transform almost every physiological and psychological system. The average American takes ten pills a day without considering it in any way radical. On the contrary, it is thought of as a form of routine maintenance, reinforcement, or defense of the body and brain. Each small local pharmacy offers thousands of substances, supplemented by rows of shelves in supermarkets, and smaller arrays in newspaper stands. This galaxy of diverse chemicals is introduced into the

body with pills, patches, drips, drops, liquids, creams, smoking, suppositories, inhalers, sprays, injections, microneedles, thin film, and pumps. The daily regime of prescription and nonprescription remedies is expanded by supplements, illegal drugs, and plants

or extracts. Local, regional, or ancient non-Western traditions guide complex regimes of absorbing substances to maintain equilibrium or respond to emergencies, social transformations, environmental shifts, cosmic events, or rituals. The chemicals from different sources and different concepts of the body and mind interact with each other in complex ways that typically lead to the introduction of still more chemicals in a kind of chain reaction.

All of these substances redesign the body, and are themselves designed, with detailed attention to the delivery systems, packaging, distribution, and promotion in vast industrialized networks, whether corporate or criminal, or networks of local knowledge, or ancient and distant traditions. There is a vast interactive metabolism linking the inside of the body with cultural and technological systems. Seen from the point of view of drugs, the human body is a porous envelope suspended in vast flows, at once transformed and stabilized by ever-shifting combinations of chemicals.

All these substances are introduced to the body in order that it can become itself again, or that it can remain being itself, or that it can become something else. Each operates in different time frames, from a simple headache for a few hours or a night's sleep, to a long-term disease. All have side effects that often lead to further substances being taken. In reaction, the body is constantly generating its own chemicals in precisely calibrated doses and locations. The sense of homeostasis is actually the product of the body rarely being the same and constantly reacting to the reactions in countless feedback loops, which includes the huge changes as it ages, during the course of each day, menstrual rhythms, awake versus sleep, resting versus active, and so on.

Can we even speak of a human without mind- and body-altering drugs? Was there ever such a thing? And wouldn't design be experienced by such a medicated being, and even be seen as another form of medication? Hasn't the human that designs, is designed for, and is designed always been chemically enhanced? Likewise, hasn't the body always been rebuilt? The continuously reconstructed body is not just the contemporary Western body in its increasingly globalized form, a consumer product whose design has to be frequently updated. Each ancient culture was defined by traditions of body modification. Redesigning the body is the very beginning of culture.

With gene-editing tools like CRISPR, the redesign of the body has moved to the genetic level. Precise insertions and deletions in a human DNA sequence can be introduced into the body to deactivate mutant genes, replace them with a healthy copy, or mobilize a new gene to fight a disease. The possibility of using these techniques on sperm or eggs to transmit the redesign to all successive generations and thereby change the human genome itself is beyond the ethical barrier for most countries. The indeterminacy of the stem cell, its ability to develop into almost any cell type, is already being used to repair organs, wounds, degenerate retinas, tendons, and teeth. The astonishing fact that human stem cells happily assist in the construction of cells of other animals, and presumably vice versa, further destabilizes the category of human with the construction of chimera, cross-species constructions at the outer limit of contemporary ethical debates. Research with part-human/part-animal embryos is exploring the possibility of growing human organs in other animals for transplant – raising multiple fears about accidentally producing human intelligence in other species and hybrid creatures that would bred with humans.

The concern about the human ability to redesign, destabilize, or destroy the balance of the planet is echoed in ethical debates about the ability to redesign gene pools. This ability has been exercised since the first domestication and redesign of animals and plants through selective breeding. But now it is radicalized with concepts like the so-called gene drive, where a genetically modified animal like a mosquito is released in order to reproduce and wipe out the species that has been modified.

Design cannot make sense without considering biodesign, the self-conscious design of new life-forms within a genetically engineered environment. With biodesign, the sense of the human redesigning itself and every element of the living environment is direct and palpable. It is as if the human brain has touched and transformed everything it encounters.

Which finally raises the question of the design of the brain itself, the very agent of design with its 100 billion neurons using around a quarter of the body's energy budget. Sebastian Seung, one of the neuroscientists leading the effort to map all the neural connections forming the "connectome," argues that simply to think is already to change the brain. Each thought adjusts the geometry of the internal forest of interconnections. The instability of the human begins with the redesign of its own brain through the very act of thinking. The idea that the human has extended its nervous system to enclose the whole planet, that artifacts are thoughts that provoke new thoughts, folds design back onto the brain itself. The vast spider's web of artifacts that have been spun out of the human body continuously reweave the internal webs of the brain. The apparent outer limits of the body are barely significant. They are just a pulsating set of porous membranes that offer no clue as to what makes the human human.

Cities were the first form of social media.
Urban density maximizes possible social
connections. You walk 100 meters from
home in a village, and you see two cows and
your grandparents. You walk 100 meters in
the city, and you have potential interactions
with 1,000 people. The fact that people
now live in a vast global spider's web of

electronic communication connected to billions of people is a continuation of the human capacity to maximize connectivity and therefore the ability to design. Social media and electronic communication is a new form of urban life. It is not simply an expansion of design. It is a revolution in the capacity to be human and inhuman.

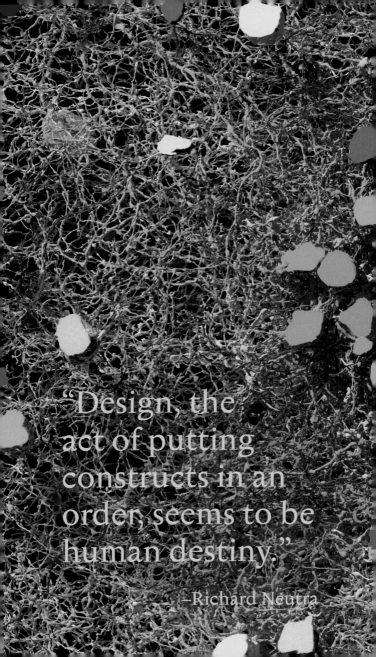

"Design, the
act of putting
constructs in an
order, seems to be
human destiny."

–Richard Neutra

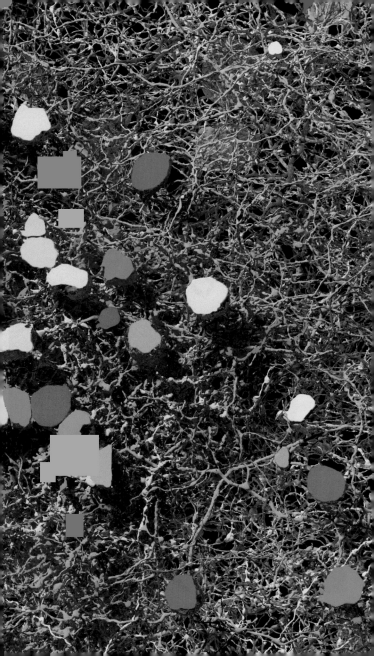

Female macaque takes a selfie, Indonesia, 2011

15

HOMO CELLULAR

Human biology and mentality was profoundly changed in 1983 by the arrival of the cell phone. The small blinking, buzzing, and beeping object in your hand might be the single prosthetic device that has done the most to transform the human.

This object has become an integral part of the body and brain. There are more active cell phones on the planet than people. Two-thirds of the world's population have at least one and more than 80 percent have access to one through sharing. More people have access to cell phones than to toilets and soon more will have phones than have electricity. The greatest acceleration in attaching phones to bodies and brains is in Asia and Africa, where already more than 40 percent of people have one. It will soon be rare to find a human without such a device. A whole new version of our species has arrived. No discussion of design can avoid this. It is not even clear that discussion of any kind is possible without engaging this redesign of the human. Perception, social interaction, memory, and even thought itself have become increasingly cellular. The device is no longer an accessory to human life but a basic of a new kind of life.

The mobile phone is usually the first thing that people touch in the morning, with a tenderness normally reserved for a baby, and the last thing they touch at night. Most sleep with their phone within arm's reach and an ever-increasing number keep it inside the bed. People feel naked, inadequate, and utterly vulnerable without their phone. It is a primary conduit of personal, social, and work life, and steadily blurs the differences between these realms. The amount of the day spent looking at the phone keeps escalating. In countries like the United States, for example, which are far from the heaviest users, people check their phone more than a hundred times a day and use it for almost five hours, with most of them underestimating the amount of time they use it by half. A recent study showed that the average person earnestly swipes, taps and pinches their phone a million times a year. More than a quarter of school-age children in South Korea use the phone for more than seven hours a day. These averages keep climbing.

The portable device is used in every possible place, in every possible hour and even plays an integral part of physical and mental life when it is not being used. The compact package of electronics is carefully deposited in bag, pocket, on the couch, lap, meal table, office desk, classroom table, exercise equipment, or bedside shelf as a key part of the person and periodically touched as if to confirm that the whole person is still there. It is checked in gaps of sleep during the night and more than a third of people admit to answering it during sex. The majority of people in the streets or moving in trains, buses, and cars have their heads permanently angled down toward the device as if engaged in some form of religious devotion. Eye contact is maintained with the phone rather than other people. It is kept constantly close at hand when not being used, ready for immediate activation in the pocket or hand bag, near the hands on the table, or remaining in the hands on the off-chance that it will become active – or

even in the hope that holding it increases the chance that
it will. The relationship is an intimate one as the object
asks for attention by vibrating, chirping, and lighting up
in response to caresses but only to your caress since it is
biometrically bonded to your fingerprints. The phone is
increasingly permanently attached to the body in earpieces,
headsets, and watches that enable communication to start
without any additional movement, just activated by voice,
but talking is an ever-smaller part of its function. It is used
for countless other tasks, developing new forms of activity
and absorbing activities that used to occur in specific
places or media like shopping, banking, mail, reading,
research, navigation, news, meetings, music, photography,
sound recording, video, games, scheduling, exercising,
note-taking, flashlight, and so on. Its huge role in relieving
boredom and avoiding communication with people in
the vicinity cannot be underestimated. The mobile phone
is both a connection and disconnection device. It is
typically placed between the human and its surroundings,

tuning the surroundings out or engaging differently with them since exhibitions, lectures, concerts, and meals are experienced more intimately, possessively, collectively, and permanently through the phone. Equally, the phone enables multiple other environments to be wrapped around the individual and choreographed in different juxtapositions. The idea that the body is in one place has gone. Even in an isolated field with the phone turned off, all the worlds that have been temporarily abandoned are palpable in their sudden absence. The empty field or dead spot in the cellular network was probably found with the phone, along with the way home.

In the end, the mobile phone is not carried, looked at, or touched by a person since the person is unthinkable without the device. A 2010 study in Britain coined the term *nomophobia* (no-mobile-phone phobia), for the distress of being without one's mobile phone, the anxiety felt by the majority of people when they forget their phone, lose reception, or the battery simply runs out. The cell phone has become part of the sense of self. The brain no longer saves the kind of information that the phone is expected to store and provide. Research on the way groups of people usually contribute different kinds of knowledge to each other in everyday life demonstrates that we now similarly offload mental capacity to the phone and even integrate the Internet into our sense of ourselves. The ability to ask questions of the phone gives the sense that the Internet is part of one's cognitive toolset.[1]

The cell phone provides new senses of both protection and vulnerability to rich and poor alike. After water and food, it is the most valued possession of the refugee, carefully wrapped in plastic for the journey, providing navigation, activating payment to smugglers, contact with friends and

family, and the archive of precious images of loved ones. The cell phone permanently attached to our body has taken over from architecture. Indeed, it has taken over much of what used to be defined as the responsibility of shelter in terms of sense of security, space, orientation, and representation.

Cell phone as shelter, then. The device offers an infinitely more complex and nuanced set of spatial conditions than those offered by traditional floors, walls, rooms, windows, streets, etc. It houses more overlapping social formations, turning traditional architectural space itself into a kind of displaced or vestigial technology. There is even an inverse relationship between the degree of privacy in traditional space and the degree of exposure online, with the maximum degree of self-exposure typically happening from the most secluded spaces – as it seems to be easier or more acceptable to show your most personal thoughts or naked body to large numbers of people at a distance than to the people nearest you. Private and public have been inverted.

The new technology takes the ability to simultaneously occupy multiple spaces that was introduced by radio at the very beginning of the twentieth century to whole new levels. It offers precise spatialities that are portable and can be combined or turned off and on or pushed to the background. It is not that physical space is unemployed. Each element of physical space now performs differently, and spaces get complicated and multiplied as they are experienced online, so the phone experience can be virtual yet can also be an experience of another physical space, and have specific impacts on those spaces.

The cell phone is the perfect example of good design, having gone through rapid evolution since the first two-and-a-half-pound *brick*← of 1983 to the superthin device of today. The external form of the brick was already designed in 1973, and was even included in a major design exhibition of portable technology in New York that year. But it took ten years and $100 million to develop and launch the technology inside it and its associated external infrastructure. The key breakthrough came another ten years later with the first smartphone, the IBM Simon (1994) with its touch screen and programs for calendar, notes, e-mail, faxes, sketchpad, maps, world clock, and news. For the first time, a computer was placed inside a phone rather than a phone inside a computer, as was eagerly reported during its launch. But this black monolith providing "total personal communications – including your cellular phone – in one small hand-held mobile device" that "works where you work, goes where you go," in the introductory words of its user manual, still weighed more than pound and could only be afforded by the rich. It

 was not until five years later that a Japanese smartphone was the first to have mass adoption in 1999, and even then the system was limited to Japan. It was only after almost twenty-five years of cell phones that the *iPhone* became the first globally adopted smartphone. This sleek device, cannily launched in June 2007 as "your life in your pocket," is like a lesson in Bauhaus design. It is smooth, integrated, lightweight, global, and efficient, with its rounded surfaces nestled in the palm of the hands, as if it is not there, as if we can touch information, and thereby touch the world.

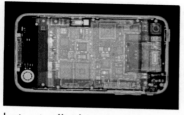

But this smoothness of good design is also an anesthetic. It numbs us to the huge changes in ourselves and our world. The cell phone tries to be as thin as it can be but actually there is nothing light or immaterial about this object. It is *densely packed*↑ with high technology and integrated into global networks sustained by vast infrastructures and economic systems. These devices have been excavated out of some of the biggest holes on the planet to gather the rare earth elements – and are produced by people working under conditions near slavery.

The cell phone is the opposite of small. The device that has so quickly become an intimate part of our body and brain is not simply a wireless interface to a hidden global infrastructure. It is itself an intimate part of that infrastructure, having rapidly evolved from a portable substitute for the fixed phone and its landlines to an interface accessing the Internet starting with the first smartphones to a vital part of the computational power of the Internet, which is not an immaterial cloud but a truly massive physical system. The cell phone is perhaps just the most visible tip of what may be the biggest human artifact of all, the global communication-computation system that literally covers the planet in an unthinkably massive material

web of webs and plays a huge role in the lives of both those who have some access to it and those who don't, yet is only experienced as a kind of ghost.

The multiple juxtaposed spaces of thought and action established by our portable devices are made possible by the invisible architecture of the cell phone concept first proposed in 1947, unpublished for twenty years, *patented in 1972←*, and finally realized in the 1980s. Closely following the original design, an invisible net of hexagon shaped "cells" now covers almost all the land of the planet with each hexagonal-space monitored by a radio tower that detects your phone and seamlessly passes your call to the next cell as you move across the invisible borders between them. In fact,

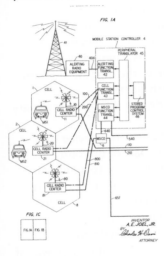

there are usually three or four overlapping nets for the different phone networks in each region, with the hexagons everywhere torqued to adjust for topography, buildings, and same-channel interference. The millions of little cell towers stitching together this invisible spatial system are in turn linked to mobile switching centers, which are linked to network switching subsystems, then local exchanges, and regional exchanges before merging with all the other kinds of communication nets to finally arrive at gargantuan server farms that are themselves tied together by fiber-optic cables passing under the oceans in a continuous web of wires and switches that effectively form vast networks of supercomputers. The largest companies have global networks of data centers, each such network having over a million interconnected servers that get activated by even the simplest question that we ask on our little phone.

This massive infrastructure that ghosts its way across the landscape is the real physical architecture through which we move. The ever-so-thin instrument now integrated into our body is no longer just a kind of interactive terminal tapping into this invisible architecture. The infrastructure is no longer imaginable without the phone. There is enormous computational force in our pocket, or rather, we are inside its pocket. Humans are attached to phones rather than phones to humans. After all, there are half a billion phones that only talk to other phones without us in continuous machine-to-machine dialogue and more than a billion are estimated to do so within a decade. The phone itself is a remarkable condensation of computational power, able to absorb a galaxy of software, and made out of elements from all over the planet. Yet it is also discarded at a rate of around two billion phones a year in the name of the latest speed and interconnectivity. The cell phone is less of an object and more like an unimaginably vast ecology combining unprecedented flows of information and material.

Cell phones are relentlessly personalized with decorative skins, wallpaper images on the screen, arrangements of favorite applications and carefully chosen images of the user, as if in response or defense against the huge scale of the device in its infrastructure, number of users, integration into countless systems, and computational power. The hidden largest artifact in human history becomes the stage of relentless personal statements by billions of people via tiny screens. Every touch of the screen becomes a statement. The number of images shared each day is around the

same number as the world population. Increasingly it is video that is shared or streamed in real time, profoundly displacing traditional institutions of publication, entertainment, journalism, art, exhibition, and law. This new way to see an ever-larger world and to be seen by ever more people is exactly that, a way to be seen ever more closely, as if the human is getting ever larger. Never has the human been placed under such relentless and precise surveillance. To say the least, the cell phone locates us in physical, personal, social, professional, commercial, and ideological space. In a sense, it knows where we are and where we might be going and with whom better than we do ourselves. This strange mirror logic finds its uncanny echo in the selfie, the fact that *Homo cellular* prefers to look backward rather than forward, to see itself embedded in its surroundings, literally using the cell phone as a mirror. This cult of self-surveillance is misunderstood as narcissism, but is more like a desperate attempt to position oneself that is now expanded by personal drones that video people from the air by following their phone.

All these acts of personal design in the face of massive invisible transnational systems are themselves integrated into those systems. The personal has become the very engine of the global ecology with every idiosyncrasy of the individual monitored and modelled. When you ask a question of your phone, the answer given is not simply to the question you ask but to the question that the real-time data analysis thinks that you are really asking, based on all the other things you are doing and have done. Your location, movements, interests, images, favorites, purchases, reading, and reactions are continuously scrutinized to produce a kind of evolving model of you. In a strange mirror logic, the phone through which you interact with the world constructs a version of you that is the real you for that world. It is not that the phone is used to monitor and accumulate details of your personal life since the phone itself is where the personal is increasingly generated. Because almost all these systems are market-driven, the cell phone tends to reinforce existing norms and inequalities. Not by chance is average income so correlated with access to the Internet and even speed of Internet. The mechanism of personal expression is equally one of normalization, reinforcing the very lines it seems to overcome.

These are the last things on our minds as we touch the device so tenderly. We don't even really want to feel how radically our body and brain has been expanded by this object. We don't want to feel the new kinds of vulnerability they bring as we put ourselves under continuous precise surveillance. And we don't really want to feel how vulnerable billions of people and the planet are, even as we watch their struggle in real time on our beautifully framed little screens. Good design is an anesthetic against the shock that design is changing us so much, changing the world so much, even that design has become the world.

An array of constantly evolving algorithms – artificial neural networks and deep learning systems – monitor every gesture we make and continuously rebuild intricate statistical images of each one of us. Each Internet search, post, transaction, and physical movement modifies this quantified human. The very fact that you are reading this sentence may be leaving a trace. Self-design turns out to be an uncanny encounter between what we offer (in the daily production of texts, comments, statements, objects, clothing choices, gestures, facial expressions, drawings, meals, exchanges, silences) and the image of ourselves that we are offered on our little screens. The algorithm shows us what it thinks we really want to see, as if in a strange kind of mirror that has become the new space of design.

"Perhaps the whole human race is only a temporally limited, developmental phase of a certain species of animal, so that man evolved from the ape and will evolve back to the ape again, while no one will be there to take any interest in this strange end of the comedy."

–Friedrich Nietzsche

Refugee's phone protected by balloon
on coast of Lesbos, 2015

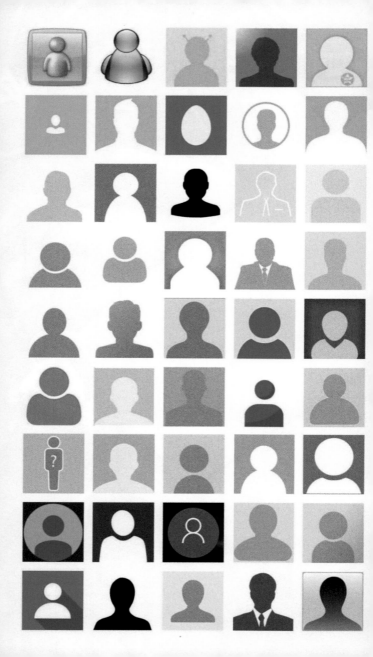

16

DESIGN
IN 2 SECONDS

Perhaps the most important transformation
in social, cultural, and economic life since
the year 2000 has been the arrival of social
media and ubiquitous surveillance culture.

Social media is the ultimate space for design, a space
where design happens at high speed by an unprecedented
number of people. Through its multiple channels we not
only communicate and collaborate with wider and wider
groups, but we refashion ourselves. Images, videos, texts,
emojis, stickers, tweets, gifs, memes, comments, posts, and
reposts are deployed to construct a very precise image,
not necessarily matching our real-life person, an avatar
launched with seemingly independent thoughts, looks,
and actions – a perfected self, perhaps the image of whom
we would like to be that becomes real online. And there
is no limit to have many digital personalities we might
maintain at the same time, including "anonymous."

There was no social media before 2000. Friends Reunited
was launched that year in Great Britain to help people locate
old school friends. This was the first successful online social
network, and by the end of the year, it had 3,000 users; a
year later, it had 2.5 million. In 2002 Friendster got 3 million
users in three months; 2003 was the year of MySpace. In
2004 Facebook started at Harvard as a collegiate version
of Friendster; within a month, half of the Harvard College
population was on it. Soon it expanded to other colleges,

and in 2005 Facebook opened to high school students. 2005 was also the year in which YouTube was launched with an invitation to "Broadcast Yourself." The year 2006 was Twitter, as well as the year in which Facebook opened to anybody above thirteen years old. WhatsApp arrived in 2009 and is the most globally popular messaging app, with 800 million users. KakaoTalk, based in Korea, was launched in 2010 and has now 140 million users. The app is used by 93 percent of smartphone owners in Korea. Instagram, launched in October 2010, had 300,000 active users as of December 2014 and 400 million in 2015. It is one of the social networks that has risen more rapidly in popularity: 53 percent of 18-to-29-year-olds use it and only 26 percent of users are older than 29. It is the more "urban," the one most used by women, Latinos, African Americans, and designers. Line, a messenger service for instant communication on electronic devices, was launched in Japan in 2011 and is also extremely popular in South Korea. It has 700 million users worldwide. It was designed by 15 members of the NHN (New Human Network) in response to Japan's devastating Tohoku earthquake in March 2011, which damaged telecommunications infrastructure.

This short history could continue, documenting all the parallel histories, in China for example, and the explosion of different forms of visual language from the dancing baby to emoticons. There has been an exponential acceleration of the number of available channels for broadcast of the self, matched by an accelerating number of people using them. There are social networks for practically everything. To find work: LinkedIn. Location-based dating apps: Tinder and Grindr. Video: Vimeo and YouTube. Mood boards: Tumblr, Pinterest. The network that has risen more rapidly among young people recently is Snapchat, where users program how long their photos and videos will be visible to other users – between 1 and 10 seconds – until permanently erased from the system. A few seconds has become a space for design.

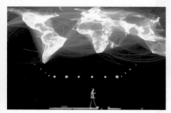

A map of Facebook users in 2010 showed 700,000 active users; there are now about *1.6 billion*←. It is estimated that 4 billion people – 60 percent of the world population – are already connected to the Internet, with 70 percent of them engaged in some form of social media, mainly through cell phones.

This represents a complete transformation of the way we live, with huge implications for architecture and design. Social media is not simply about what occurs in digital space – constructing a new kind of virtual city that has taken over many of the functions of the traditional city. We now inhabit a kind of hybrid space between the virtual and the real. Social media also redefines and restructures physical space, the space of our homes and cities. As with the arrival of mass media in the early twentieth century, social media redraws once again what is public and what is private, what is inside and what is outside. Design in the age of social media is not just what occurs in the space of a

little screen. Social media redesigns the space we live in.

Early twentieth-century architects lamented the effect of photography and the illustrated journal on architecture. Adolf Loos, for example, criticized his contemporary and rival Austrian architect Josef Hoffmann because in Loos's view his houses appeared to be made for the camera. They were two-dimensional and had lost all tectonic qualities. It was difficult to tell them apart in photographs from their cardboard models. Loos was proud of the fact that his clients could not recognize their own houses in photographs.

A new generation of architects is now being asked by their young clients to design spaces that will look good on Facebook, Instagram, YouTube, etc. Even competitions, such as the MoMA PS1 Young Architects pavilion, take into consideration how "Instagramable" the winning design

Kakao Friends

will be. Any building will be experienced far more often in social media than in the streets and the encounter in the street is already shaped by social media. Social media is not simply the posting and sharing of things that have occurred. Rather, the experience occurs within the environment of sharing. While a generation ago design concerned itself with its reception in the printed press (newspapers, professional journals, magazines) now the concern is rather reception in social media. How many tweets, how many likes, how many followers, how many reposts: the ultimate goal is design going viral.

It is not simply the expansion of reception that matters here. The Internet and social media are fundamentally redefining the spaces in which we live, our relationship to objects and to each other. Social media is a new form of urbanization, the architecture of how we live together. In what is probably now a conservative estimate, the *Wall Street Journal* reported in 2012 that 80 percent of young New York City professionals *work regularly from bed↓*. The fantasy of the home office has given way to the reality of the bed office. The very meaning of the word *office* has

been transformed. Millions of dispersed beds are taking over from concentrated office buildings. The boudoir is defeating the tower. Networked electronic technologies have removed any limit to what can be done in bed.

How did we get here?

In his famous short text "Louis-Philippe, or the Interior," Walter Benjamin wrote of the splitting of work and home in the nineteenth century:

> Under Louis-Philippe, the private citizen enters the stage of history. . . . For the private person, living space becomes, for the first time, antithetical to the place of work. The former is constituted by the interior; the office is its complement. The private person who squares his accounts with reality in his office demands that his interior be maintained in his illusions. . . . From this spring the phantasmagorias of the interior. For the private individual the private environment represents the universe. In it he gathers remote places and the past. His living room is a box in the world theater.[1]

Industrialization brought with it the eight-hour shift and the radical separation between the home and the office or factory, between rest and work, night and day. Postindustrialization collapses work back into the home and takes it further into the bedroom and into the bed itself. Phantasmagoria is no longer lining the room in wallpaper, fabric, images, and objects. It is now in electronic devices. The whole universe is concentrated on a small screen with the bed floating in an infinite sea of information. To lie down is not to rest but to move. The bed is now a site of action. But the voluntary invalid has

no need of their legs. The bed has become the ultimate prosthetic and a whole new industry is devoted to providing contraptions to facilitate work while lying down – reading, writing, texting, recording, broadcasting, listening, talking, and, of course, eating, drinking, sleeping, or making love, activities that seem to have been turned, of late, into work itself. Waiters in restaurants in the United States ask if you are "still working on that" before removing your plate or your glass. Endless advice is dispensed about how to "work" on your personal relationships, "schedule" sex with your partner. Sleeping is definitely hard work too, for millions, with the psychopharmaceutical industry providing new drugs every year and an army of sleep experts providing advice on how to achieve this apparently ever more elusive goal – all in the name of higher productivity, of course. Everything done in the bed has become work.

This philosophy was already embodied in the figure of *Hugh Hefner*←, who famously almost never left his bed, let alone his house. He literally moved his office to his bed in 1960 when he moved into the Playboy Mansion at 1340 North State Parkway, Chicago, turning it into the epicenter of a global empire and his silk pajamas and dressing gown into his business attire. "I don't go out of the house at all!!! . . . I am a contemporary recluse," he told Tom Wolfe, guessing that the last time he was out had been three and a half months before and that in the last two years he had been out of the house only nine times.[2] Fascinated, Wolfe described him as "the tender-tympany green heart of an artichoke."[3]

Playboy turns the bed into a workplace. From the mid-1950s on, the bed becomes increasingly sophisticated, outfitted with all sorts of entertainment and communication devices as a kind of control room.

Hefner was not alone. The bed may have been the ultimate American office at midcentury. In an interview in the *Paris Review* in 1957, Truman Capote is asked, "What are some of your writing habits? Do you use a desk? Do you write on a machine?" To which he answers: "I am a completely horizontal author. I can't think unless I'm lying down, either in bed or stretched on a couch and with a cigarette and a coffee handy."[4]

Even architects set up office in bed at midcentury. Richard Neutra started working the moment he woke up with elaborate equipment enabling him to design, write, or even interview in bed. As his son Dion Neutra revealed:

> Dad's best time for creative thinking was early in the morning, long before any activity had started in the office below. He often stayed in bed working with ideas and designs, even extending into appointments which had been made earlier. His one concession to convention was to put on a tie over his night shirt when receiving visitors while still propped up in bed![5]

Neutra's bed↗ in the VDL house in Silver Lake, Los Angeles, included two public phones; three communication stations for talking with other rooms in the house, the office below, and even another office 500 meters away; three different call bells; drafting boards and easels that folded down over the bed; electric lights and a radio-gramophone controlled from a dashboard overhead. A bedside table rolling on casters held the tape recorder, electric clock, and storage compartments for drawing and writing equipment so that he could, as Neutra put it in a letter to his sister, "use every minute from morning to late night."[6]

Postwar America inaugurated the high-performance bed as an epicenter of productivity, a new form of industrialization that was exported globally and has now become available to an international army of dispersed but interconnected producers. A new kind of factory without walls is constructed by compact electronics and extra pillows for the 24/7 generation.

The kind of equipment that Hefner envisioned (some of which, like the answering machine, didn't yet exist) is now expanded for the Internet and social media generation, who not only work in bed but socialize in bed, exercise in bed, read the news in bed, and entertain sexual relationships with people miles away from their beds. The *Playboy* fantasy of the nice girl next door is more likely realized today with someone on another continent than in the same building or neighborhood – a person you may have never seen before and may never see again, and it is anybody's guess if she is real (as in, exists in some place and time) or an electronic construction. Does it matter? As in the recent film *Her*, a moving depiction of life in the soft, uterine state that is a corollary to our new mobile

technologies, the "her" in question is an operating system that turns out to be a more satisfying partner than a person. The protagonist lies in bed with Her, chatting, arguing, making love and eventually breaking up still in bed.

If, according to Jonathan Crary, late capitalism is the end of sleep, colonizing every minute of our lives for production and consumption, the actions of the voluntary recluse are not so voluntary in the end.[7] The nineteenth-century division of the city between rest and work may soon become obsolete. Not only have our habits and habitat changed with the Internet and social media, but the predictions about the end of human labor in the wake of new technologies and robotization that were already being made at the end of the nineteenth century are no longer treated as futuristic. Thirty-five years ago, the late economist Wassily Leontief said "They replaced horses, didn't they?" and the business section of *The New York Times* recently reconsidered his idea of the end of the "human workhouse":

> Horses hung around in the labor force for quite some time after they were first challenged by "modern" communications technologies like the telegraph and the railroad, hauling stuff and people around farms and cities. But when the internal combustion engine came along, horses – as a critical component of the world economy – were history.... Humans as workhorses might also be on the way out.[8]

Economists wonder what kind of economic model this reality will lead to: from growing inequalities with vast amount of people unemployed to large-scale redistribution in the form of Universal Basic Income, which was recently considered in a referendum in Switzerland and rejected. The end of paid labor and its replacement with creative leisure was already envisioned in utopian projects of the 1960s and 1970s by Constant, Superstudio, and Archigram, including hyperequipped beds. Meanwhile the city has started to redesign itself.

In today's attention-deficit-disorder society, we have discovered that we work better in short bursts punctuated by rest. Today many companies provide sleeping pods in the office to maximize productivity. Bed and office are never far apart in the 24/7 world. Special self-enclosed beds have been designed for office spaces – turning themselves into compact sealed capsules, minispaceships, that can be used in isolation or gathered together in clusters or lined up in rows for synchronized sleep – understood as a part of work rather than its opposite.

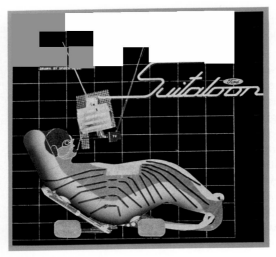

Michael Webb, Suitaloon, 1968

Between the bed inserted in the office and the office inserted in the bed a whole new horizontal architecture has taken over. It is magnified by the "flat" networks of social media that have themselves been fully integrated into the professional, business, and industrial environment in a collapse of traditional distinctions between private and public, work and play, rest and action. The bed itself – with its ever more sophisticated mattress, linings, and technical attachments – is the basis of an intrauterine environment that combines the sense of deep interiority with the sense of hyperconnectivity to the outside.

What is the nature of this new interior in which we have decided collectively to check ourselves in? What is the architecture of this prison in which night and day, work and play are no longer differentiated and we are permanently under surveillance? New media turns us

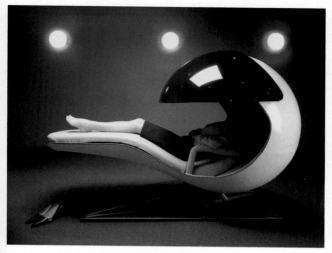

MetroNaps sleeping pod, 2014

all into inmates, constantly under surveillance, even as we celebrate endless connectivity. We have all become "a contemporary recluse," as Hugh Hefner put it a half a century ago.

In Laura Poitras's film *Citizenfour*, we see Edward Snowden close up, sitting on his bed in a Hong Kong hotel for days on end, surrounded by his laptops, communicating with journalists in the room and around the world about the secret world of massive global surveillance. The biggest invasion of privacy in the history of the planet is revealed from bed and dominates all media. The most public figure in the world at that moment is a recluse. Architecture has been inverted.

Writers and artists in the twentieth century worked from bed, from Proust to Matisse, to Truman Capote, who couldn't even think unless he was lying down. Today

Edward Snowden in *Citizenfour*

everybody is an artist, a writer, a curator, a designer. . . . If Walter Benjamin thought the arrival of the printing press made everyone a critic, the arrival of social media makes everyone an author, an artist, a self-designer. One of the paradoxes of the age of social media and the sharing economy is the extreme cultivation of the sense of self. Everybody has the fantasy of being an independent producer, self-employed in the permanent project of constructing oneself. Self-design has become the main responsibility and activity. As Boris Groys writes:

> With the death of God, design became the medium of the soul, the revelation of the subject hidden inside the human body. Thus design took on an ethical dimension it had not had previously. In design, ethics became aesthetics; it became form. Where religion once was, design has emerged. The modern subject now has a new obligation: the obligation to self-design, an aesthetic presentation as ethical subject.[9]

Social media appears to have been constructed for this task. It is not simply that social media is a tool for self-design. Self-design has become media. This designing self is not an independent inventive subject or collective. It is an always fragile work-in-progress, sacrificing all privacy to produce big data in return for a new illusion of independence.

Design is never quite what it claims to be. Fortunately. Its attempt to smooth over all the worries and minimize any friction always fails, in the same way that almost every minute of daily life is organized by the unsuccessful attempt to bury the unconscious. We need to put design on the couch. Design is filled by what it wants to hide. The simple question *are we human?* is just a way to say *what is design?* until the confessions and the fantasies come out.

Endnotes

1. John Evans, "On the Occurrence of Flint Implements in Undisturbed Beds of Gravel, Sand, and Clay," paper read June 2, 1859, *Archaeologia* 38, no. 2 (January 1861).

2. Joseph Prestwich, "On the Occurrence of Flint Implements Associated with the Remains of Animals of Extinct Species in Beds of a Late Geological Period in France at Amiens and Abbeville and in England at Hoxne," paper read May 26, 1859, in *Philosophical Transactions of the Royal Society of London* 150 (1860): 294.

3. Evans, "On the Occurrence of Flint Implements," 306 (see note 1).

4. Charles Darwin, *On the Origin of Species by Means of Natural Selection* (London: John Murray, 1859), 189. Darwin was directly countering William Paley's argument that there is no design without a designer, which used the extended example of the eye and the telescope. William Paley, *Natural Theology* (London: R. Faulder, 1802), 19.

5. Charles Darwin, *The Descent of Man in Relationship to Sex* (London: John Murray, 1871), 3.

6. Ibid., 138. See also Alastair J. M. Key and Stephen J. Lycett, "Technology Based Evolution? A Biometric Test of the Effects of Handsize Versus Tool Form on Efficiency in an Experimental Cutting Task," *Journal of Archaeological Science* 38, no. 7 (2011): 1663–70.

7. Mary W. Marzke, "Tool Making, Hand Morphology and Fossil Hominins," *Philosophical Transactions of the Royal Society*, no. 368 (October 2013).

8. *Paris Universal Exposition, 1867. Reports of the United States Commissioners*, vol. 1 (Washington, DC: US Senate, 1870), 17.

9. John Frere, "Account of Flint Weapons Discovered at Hoxne in Suffolk," *Archaeologia* 13 (January 1800): 205.

10. Jacque Boucher de Perthes, *Antiquités celtiques et antédiluviennes. Mémoire sur l'industrie primitive et les arts à leur origine* (Paris: Treuttel et Wurtz, 1847).

11. Clive Gamble and Robert Kruszynski, "John Evans, Joseph Prestwich and the Stone that Shattered the Time Barrier," *Antiquity* 83, no. 320 (June 2009): 461–75.

12. Prestwich, "On the Occurrence of Flint Implements," 293 (see note 2).

13. Charles Darwin to J. D. Hooker, 22 June 1859, in *The Correspondence of Charles Darwin*, vol. 7, ed. Frederick Burkhardt and Sydney Smith (Cambridge: Cambridge University Press, 1991), 308. On July 2, he told Hooker, "I have much idle curiosity on the Human tools, & am glad to hear that you think them

certainly human: their number makes the case wonderfully curious." Ibid., 316.

14. Charles Darwin, *On the Origin of Species by Means of Natural Selection* (New York: D. Appleton, 1861), 23.

15. Charles Darwin, *The Descent of Man in Relationship to Sex* (New York: D. Appleton, 1861), 53.

16. Ibid., 377.

THE INVENTION OF THE HUMAN

1. Bernard Stiegler, *Technics and Time, 1: The Fault of Epimetheus*, trans. Richard Beardsworth and George Collins (Stanford: Stanford University Press, 1998), 152.

2. André Leroi-Gourhan, *Speech and Gesture*, trans. Anna Bostock Berger (Cambridge, MA: MIT Press, 1993), 235. Originally published as *Le Geste et la parole* (1964).

3. Ibid., 240.

4. Lambros Malafouris, *How Things Shape the Mind: A Theory of Material Engagement* (Cambridge, MA: MIT Press, 2013), 169. "The directed action of stone knapping does not simply execute but rather *brings forth* the knapper's intention.... The stone, like the knapper's body, is an integral and complementary part of the intention to knap. In the case of knapping, intentionality is not a property that stops at the boundary of the biological organism...sometimes the stone becomes the 'extension' of the knapper. At other times, however, the knapper becomes the 'extension' of the stone." Ibid., 173–76.

5. John J. Shea, "Refuting a Myth about Human Origins," *American Scientist* 99 (March–April 2011): 128–35. "Hominoid evolution has...yielded species that excel in behavioural novelty, diversity, and highly sophisticated use of environmental data. With its metabolically expensive brain and sophisticated social networks, *Homo sapiens* is an extreme example of the latter type of species." See also Richard Potts, "Variability Selection in Hominid Evolution," *Evolutionary Anthropology* 7 (1998): 81–96.

6. Kim Sterelny, "From Hominin to Humans: How *sapiens* Became Behaviourally Modern," *Philosophical Transactions of the Royal Society* (2011): 809–22.

7. Patrick Roberts, "'We Have Never Been Behaviourally Modern': The Implications of Material Engagement Theory and Metaplasticity for Understanding the Late Pleistocene Record of Human Behaviour," *Quaternary International* 30 (2015): 5.

THE ORNAMENTAL SPECIES

1. John F. Hoffecker, *Landscape of the Mind: Human Evolution and the Archaeology of Thought* (New York: Columbia University Press, 2011), 6.

2. Maxime Aubert et al., "Pleistocene Cave Art from Sulawesi, Indonesia," *Nature* 514 (October 9, 2014): 223–27.

3. Steven L. Kuhn and Mary C. Siner, "Body Ornamentation as Information Technology: Towards an Understanding of the Significance of Early Beads," in *Rethinking the Human Revolution: New Behavioural and Biological Perspectives on the Origin and Dispersal of Modern Humans*, ed. Paul Mellars et al. (Cambridge: McDonald Institute for Archaeological Research, 2007), 47.

4. Marian Vanhaeran et al., "Middle Paleolithic Shell Beads in Israel and Algeria," *Science* 312 (2006): 1786.

5. Marek Kohn and Steven Mithen, "Handaxes: Products of Sexual Selection?," *Antiquity* 73, no. 281 (September 1999): 518–26.

6. Hoffecker, *Landscape of the Mind*, 53 (see note 1).

7. Ibid., 139.

8. Slavoj Zizek, "Design as an Ideological State-Apparatus," in *Designing Everyday Life*, ed. Jan Boelen and Vera Sacchetti (Ljubljana: Museum of Architecture and Design, 2014), 68.

9. Ian Watts, "Early Color Symbolism," in *Handbook of Color Psychology*, ed. Andrew J. Elliot, Mark D. Fairchild, and Anna Franklin (Cambridge: Cambridge University Press, 2015), 329.

10. Marian Vanhaeren et al., "Thinking Strings: Additional Evidence for Personal Ornament Use in the Middle Stone Age at Blombos Cave, South Africa," *Journal of Human Evolution* 64, no. 6 (June 2013): 500–517.

11. Mary C. Stiner, Steven L. Kuhn, and Erksin Güleç, "Early Upper Paleolithic Shell Beads at Üçağızlı Cave I (Turkey): Technology and the Socioeconomic Context of Ornament Life-Histories," *Journal of Human Evolution* 64, no. 5 (May 2013): 380–98.

NEWS FROM NOWHERE

1. Samuel Butler, "Darwin among the Machines [To the Editor of the Press, Christchurch, New Zealand, 13 June 1863]," in *A First Year in Canterbury Settlement with Other Early Essays* (London: A. C. Fifield, 1914), 182.

2. *Report from the Select Committee on Arts and Their Connection with Manufactures* (London: Luke Hansard, 1836).

3. Henry Cole and Richard Redgrave, eds.,

Journal of Design and Manufactures 1, no. 1 (March 1849): 1.

4. Henry Cole and Richard Redgrave, eds., *Journal of Design and Manufactures* 4, no. 19 (September 1, 1850): 9.

5. William Morris, "The Aims of Art (1886)," in *Signs of Change: Lectures on Socialism*, vol. 23 of *The Collected Works of William Morris* (New York: Russell and Russell, 1966), 87.

6. Charles Harvey and Jon Press, "William Morris and the Royal Commission on Technical Instruction, 1881–1884," *Journal of William Morris Studies* 11, no. 1 (Autumn 1994): 35.

7. William Morris, "News from Nowhere," first published in serialized form from January 11, 1890, in *Commonweal*.

8. Hermann Muthesius, *Style-Architecture and Building-Art: Transformations of Architecture in the Nineteenth Century and Its Present Condition*, trans. Stanford Anderson (Los Angeles: Getty Research Institute, 1994), 91; originally published in 1902 as *Stilarchitektur und Baukunst*.

9. Adolf Behne, *The Modern Functional Building*, trans. Michael Robinson (Los Angeles: Getty Research Institute, 1996), 128; originally published in 1926 as *Der Moderne Zweckbau*.

10. Ibid., 87.

11. Ibid., 123.

GOOD DESIGN IS AN ANESTHETIC

1. Alfred Lichtwark, "Wandlungen (1894)," in *Palastfenster und Flügeltür*, 3rd ed. (Berlin: Bruno Cassirer, 1905), 148.

2. Adolf Loos, "The Leather Goods, and Gold- and Silversmiths Trades," trans. J. O. Newman and J. H. Smith, in *Spoken into the Void: Collected Essays, 1897–1900*, (Cambridge, MA: MIT Press, 1983), 7–9.

3. Hermann Muthesius, "New Ornament and New Art," trans. Annika Fisher, in *West 86th: A Journal of Decorative Arts, Design History, and Material Culture* 22, no. 1 (March 2015): 77–84.

4. Adolf Loos, "Ornament and Crime," in *The Architecture of Adolf Loos: An Arts Council Exhibition*, ed. Yehuda Safran and Wilfried Wang (London: The Arts Council of Great Britain, 1985).

5. Le Corbusier, *Toward an Architecture*, trans. John Goodman (Los Angeles: Getty Research Institute, 2007), 150. Originally published in 1923 as *Vers une architecture*.

6. Le Corbusier, *L'Almanach d'architecture moderne* (Paris: Crès, 1924), 21.

7. Robert Mallet-Stevens, "Architecture and Geometry (1924)," trans. Charlotte Benton and Tim Benton, in *Architecture and Design, 1890–1939: An International Anthology of Original Articles* (New York: Whitney Museum, 1975), 131.

8. "Exhibition of Useful Objects Under Five Dollars," MoMA press release, 1938.

9. "'Command Performance' for Pots and Pans, Ash Trays, Lamps, Waste Baskets, and Other Household Objects," MoMA press release for *Useful Objects Under $10* exhibition, 1941.

10. Le Corbusier, *The Decorative Art of Today*, trans. James I. Dunnett (Cambridge, MA: MIT Press, 1987), 96. See also Nina Rosenblatt, "Empathy and Anaesthesia: On the Origins of a French Machine Aesthetic," *Grey Room*, no. 2 (Winter 2001), 78–97. Originally published in 1925 as *L'Art décoratif d'aujourd'hui*.

11. Le Corbusier, *The Decorative Art of Today*, 112 (see note 10).

12. Walter Benjamin, "Experience and Poverty," trans. Rodney Livingstone, in *Walter Benjamin: Selected Writings Vol. 2: 1927–34*, ed. Marcus Bullock and Michael W. Jennings (Cambridge, MA: Belknap Press, 1999), 732.

13. Walter Benjamin, *Charles Baudelaire*, trans. Harry Zohn (London: Verso, 1983), 133.

14. Susan Buck Mors, "Aesthetics and Anaesthetics: Walter Benjamin's Artwork Essay Reconsidered," *October* 62 (Fall 1992): 3–42.

15. Walter Benjamin, "On Some Motifs on Baudelaire," *Illuminations* (New York: Harcourt, Brace &World, 1968), 155.

16. Adolf Loos, "Architecture" in *The Architecture of Adolf Loos*, 107 (see note 4).

17. Adolf Loos, "Die englische Uniform," *Neues 8 Uhr-Blatt*, May 24, 1919.

18. Adolf Loos, "Wohnen lernen!" *Neues Wiener Tagblatt*, May 15, 1921. Loos cites landscape architect Leberecht Migge about men who possess modern nerves.

19. Adolf Loos, "Ornament und Erziehung" (1924), in *Sämtliche Schriften*, ed. Frank Glück, 2 vols. (Vienna: Herold, 1962), 1:392–93.

20. Walter Benjamin, "Karl Kraus," in *Walter Benjamin: Selected Writings, Vol. 2: 1927–34*, 433–58 (see note 12).

21. Buckminster Fuller, "Universal Conditions of the Industrially Reproducible Shelter," *T-Square* 2, no. 2 (February 1932): 37.

22. "Case Study Houses 8 and 9 by Charles Eames and Eero Saarinen, Architects," *Arts & Architecture* (December 1949): 43.

THE DESIGN OF HEALTH

1. Vitruvius Pollio, *The Ten Books on Architecture*, trans. Morris Hicky Morgan (Cambridge, MA: Harvard University Press, 1914), 20.

2. Austin Flint and William H. Welch, *The Principles and Practice of Medicine*, 5th ed. (Philadelphia: Henry C. Lea's Son & Co., 1881), 206. See also Susan Sontag, *Illness as Metaphor* (New York: Vintage Books, 1979), 54.

3. Sontag, *Illness as Metaphor*, 5 (see note 2).

4. Anson Rabinbach, *The Human Motor: Energy, Fatigue, and the Origins of Modernity* (New York: Basic Books, 1990).

5. Le Corbusier, *Toward an Architecture*, trans. John Goodman (Los Angeles: Getty Research Institute, 2007), 94–95. Originally published in 1923 as *Vers une architecture*.

6. Dr. Winter, "Sport," *L'Esprit nouveau*, no. 16 (May 1922): 1952.

7. Dr. Winter, "Le Corps nouveau," *L'Esprit nouveau*, no. 15 (Feb. 1922): 1755.

8. Le Corbusier, *The City of To-morrow and Its Planning*, trans. Frederick Etchells (New York: Dover Editions, 1987), 84; originally published in 1925 as *Urbanisme*; and *The Radiant City*, trans. Pamela Knight, Eleanor Levieux, and Derek Coltman (New York: Orion Press, 1967), 36; originally published in 1933 as *La Ville Radieuse*.

9. Richard Neutra, *Survival through Design* (New York: Oxford University Press, 1953), 194.

10. Dodie Bellamy, "When the Sick Rule the World," *When the Sick Rule the World* (South Pasadena: Semiotext(e), 2015), 35.

HUMAN-CENTERED DESIGN

1. R. M. Schindler, "Modern Architecture: A Program (1912)," in David Gebhard, *Schindler* (New York: Viking Press, 1972), 192.

2. Eileen Gray and Jean Badovici, "Maison en bord de mer," *L'Architecture vivante* (Winter 1929). Translated in Caroline Constant, *Eileen Gray* (London: Phaidon, 2000), 238.

3. Le Corbusier, *The Decorative Art of Today*, trans. James Dunnett (Cambridge, MA: MIT Press, 1987), 72. Originally published in 1925 as *L'Art décoratif d'aujourd'hui*.

4. Ibid., 110.

5. Hannes Meyer, "The New World (1926)," in *Hannes Meyer: Buildings, Projects and Writings*, ed. Claude Schnaidt, trans. D. Q. Stephenson (New York: Architectural Book Publishing, 1965), 91–95.

6. Hannes Meyer, "Building (1928,)" in *Programs and Manifestoes on Twentieth-Century Architecture*, ed. Ulrich Conrads (Cambridge, MA: MIT Press, 1964), 117–20.

7. Buckminster Fuller, *Nine Chains to the Moon* (Philadelphia: Lippincott, 1938).

8. Max Bill, "Beauty from Function and As Function," lecture to Swiss Werkbund on October 23, 1948, in *Max Bill's View of Things: Die Gute Form: An Exhibition 1949* (Zurich: Lars Müller Publishers, 2015), 144.

9. Richard Neutra, *Survival Through Design* (New York: Oxford University Press, 1954), 3.

10. Lina Bo Bardi, "The Moon (1958)," in *Stones Against Diamonds* (London: Architectural Association, 2012), 64.

11. Sigfried Giedion, *Mechanization Takes Command: A Contribution to Anonymous History* (New York: Oxford University Press, 1948), 723.

12. Sigfried Giedion, *The Eternal Present: The Beginnings of Art* (New York: Bollingen Foundation, 1962), xix.

13. See Joseph Rykwert, *On Adam's House in Paradise: The Idea of the Primitive Hut in Architectural Theory* (New York: Museum of Modern Art, 1972).

14. Bernard Rudofsky, *Architecture Without Architects* (New York: Museum of Modern Art, 1965), 2.

15. Hans Hollein, ed., *Man TransFORMS* (New York: Cooper Hewitt Museum, 1976).

THE FRICTIONLESS SILHOUETTE

1. Vitruvius Pollio, *The Ten Books on Architecture*, trans. Morris Hicky Morgan (Cambridge, MA: Harvard University Press, 1914), 72.

2. Ernst Neufert, *Der Mensch als Mass und Ziel* (Berlin: Bauwelt-Verlag, 1935).

3. Ernst Neufert, *Bau-Entwurfslehre* (Berlin: Bauwelt-Verlag, 1936).

4. Étienne-Jules Marey, *La Machine animale: Locomotion terrestre et aérienne* (Paris: G. Baillière, 1873).

5. Frederick Winslow Taylor, *The Principals of Scientific Management* (New York: Harper, 1911).

6. Aleksei Gastev, "Nashi Zadachi" (1921), cited in Kendall E. Bailes, "Alexei Gastev and the Soviet Controversy Over Taylorism, 1918–1924," *Soviet Studies* 39, no. 3 (July 1977): 373–94.

7. Oskar Schlemmer, *Man: Teaching Notes from the Bauhaus* (Cambridge, MA: MIT Press, 1971).

8. Oskar Schlemmer to Otto Meyer, 3 February 1921, in *The Letters and Diaries of Oskar Schlemmer*, ed. Tut Schlemmer (Middletown, CT: Wesleyan University Press, 1972), 98.

9. Frederick Kiesler, "On Correalism and Biotechnique: A Definition and Test of a New Approach to Building Design,"

Architectural Record 86, no. 3, *On Correalism and Biotechnique* (September 1939): 60–75.

10. Le Corbusier, *Le Modulor. Essai sur une mesure harmonique à l'échelle humaine, applicable universellement à l'architecture et à la mécanique* (Boulogne: Éditions de l'Architecture d'aujourd'hui, 1951).

11. Le Corbusier, *Modulor 2* (Boulogne: Éditions de l'Architecture d'aujourd'hui, 1955).

12. Henry Dreyfuss, *Designing for People* (New York: Simon and Schuster, 1955).

13. Henry Dreyfuss, *The Measure of Man: Human Factors in Design* (New York: Whitney Library of Design, 1959).

DESIGNING THE BODY

1. OMA/Office for Metropolitan Architecture, "La Casa Palestra," *AA Files*, no. 13 (1987): 8.

2. Willard Morgan, "Plumbing and Heating for a Modern Health Home," *Domestic Engineering* (April 5, 1930): 52.

3. Philip Lovell, "Care of the Body," *Los Angeles Times Sunday Magazine*, December 15, 1929, 26.

4. Philip Lovell and Leah Lovell, *Diet for Health by Natural Methods* (Los Angeles: Times-Mirror Press, 1927), 16. Quoted in Victoria Jane Solan, "Built for Health" (PhD diss., Yale University, 2004), 140.

5. Neutra quoted by Solan, 145–46 (see note 4).

6. Sara Schrank, "Naked Houses: The Architecture of Nudism and the Rethinking of the American Suburb," *Journal of Urban History* 38, no. 4 (2012): 638.

7. Sylvia Lavin, *Form Follows Libido: Architecture and Richard Neutra in a Psychoanalytic Culture* (Cambridge, MA: MIT Press, 2004), 76.

8. Frederick Kiesler, "Pseudo-Functionalism in Modern Architecture," *Partisan Review* (July 1949): 735. Emphasis in the original.

9. Ibid., 739.

10. Thomas Creighton, "Kiesler's Pursuit of an Idea," *Progressive Architecture* 42, no. 7 (1961): 106.

DESIGN AS PERVERSION

1. Felicity Scott, "Underneath Aesthetics and Utility: The Untransposable Fetish of Bernard Rudofsky," *Assemblage* 38 (April 1999).

2. Press release for *Are Clothes Modern*, including "Partial List of Labels," MoMA, November 27, 1944.

3. Scott, "Underneath Aesthetics and Utility," 73 (see note 1).

4. Bernard Rudofsky, *Are Clothes Modern* (Chicago: P. Theobald, 1947), 175.

5. Ibid., 176. Rudofsky is referring here to Sigmund Freud, "Fetischismus," *Internationale Zeitschrift für Psychoanalyse* 4 (1927): 373.

6. Bernard Tschumi, "Violence of Architecture," *Artforum* (September 1981): 44–46.

7. Beatriz Colomina, "A House of Ill Repute: E. 1027," in *Interiors*, ed. Johanna Burton, Lynne Cooke, and Josiah McElheny (Annandale-on-Hudson, NY: Center for Curatorial Studies, Bard College; Berlin: Sternberg Press, 2012).

8. Samir Rafi, "Le Corbusier et 'les femmes d'Alger,'" *Revue d'histoire et de civilisation du Maghreb* (Algiers) (January 1968): 51.

9. Ibid. From several conversations of both Le Corbusier and Ozenfant with Samir Rafi in 1964.

10. In his book *My Work*, Le Corbusier refers to the mural as *Graffiti at Cap Martin*. In "Le Corbusier as Painter," Stanislaus von Moos labels the mural *Three Women (Graffite à Cap Martin)*, and in "Le Corbusier et 'les femmes d'Alger,'" Samir Rafi labels the final composition from which the mural was derived *Assemblage des trois femmes: Composition définitive*. Encre de Chine sur papier calque. 49.7 × 64.4 cm. Coll. particulière. Milan.

11. Letter from Marie Louise Schelbert (who bought E.1027 after the death of Badovici) to Stanislaus von Moos, February 14, 1969, quoted by von Moos, in "Le Corbusier as Painter," *Oppositions* 19–20 (1980): 93.

12. Adolf Loos, "The Plumbers," in *Spoken into the Void*, trans. Jane O. Newman and John H. Smith (Cambridge, MA: MIT Press, 1982), 45–46.

13. Beatrice Wood, *The Blind Man* 2 (1917).

14. "Demand a bathroom in full sunlight, one of the largest rooms in the apartment, the old drawing room for example. I don't know why in modern French a toilet is called a closet; the days of the clyster pipe [enema tube] are long gone." Le Corbusier, *Toward an Architecture*, trans. John Goodman (Los Angeles: Getty Publications, 2007), 172; originally published in 1923 as *Vers une architecture*.

15. *Das Werk*, no. 19 (1927): 263. Cited in Karin Kirsch, *The Weissenhofsiedlung: Experimental Housing Built for the Deutscher Werkbund, Stuttgart, 1927* (New York: Rizzoli, 1989), 118.

DESIGNING A GHOST

1. *Ja! Stimmen des Arbeitsrates für Kunst* (Berlin: Arbeitsrat für Kunst, 1919), 32.
2. Walter Gropius, *The New Architecture and the Bauhaus*, trans. P. Morton Shand (Cambridge, MA: MIT Press, 1965), 48.
3. Ibid., 33.
4. Walter Gropius, *Internationale Architektur* (Munich: A. Langen, 1925).
5. Adolf Behne, *The Modern Functional Building*, trans. Michael Robinson (Los Angeles: Getty Research Institute, 1996), originally published in 1926 as *Der Moderne Zweckbau*.

THE UNSTABLE BODY

1. See Ruth E. Ley et al., "Evolution of Mammals and their Gut Microbes," *Science* 320 (June 20 2008): 1647–51: and Andrew H. Moeller et al., "Cospeciation of Gut Microbiota with Hominids," *Science* 353 (July 22, 2016): 380–82.
2. Alastair Crisp et al., "Expression of Multiple Horizontally Acquired Genes is a Hallmark of Both Vertebrate and Invertebrate Genomes," *Genome Biology* 16:50 (2015), doi 10.1186/s13059-015-0607-3.

HOMO CELLULAR

1. Daniel M. Wegner and Adrian F. Ward, "How Google Is Changing Your Brain," *Scientific American* 309, no. 6 (2013): 58–61.

DESIGN IN 2 SECONDS

2. Walter Benjamin, "Louis-Philippe, or the Interior," in *Reflections: Essays, Aphorisms, Autobiographical Writings*, ed. Peter Demetz, trans. Edmund Jephcott (New York: Schoken Books, 1978), 154.
3. Tom Wolfe, "King of the Status Dropouts," *The Pump House Gang* (New York: Farrar, Straus & Giroux, 1965).
4. Ibid., 63.
5. "Truman Capote, The Art of Fiction No. 17," interviewed by Patti Hill, *The Paris Review* 16 (Spring–Summer 1957).
6. Dion Neutra, "The Neutra Genius: Innovation and Vision," *Modernism* 1, no. 3 (December 1998).
7. Richard Neutra to Verena Saslavsky, 4 December 1953, Dion Neutra Papers, quoted in Thomas S. Hines, *Richard Neutra and the Search for Modern Architecture: A Biography and History* (Los Angeles: University of California Press, 1982), 251.
8. Jonathan Crary, *24/7: Late Capitalism and the Ends of Sleep* (New York: Verso, 2013).
9. Eduardo Porter, "Contemplating the End of the Human Workhorse," *The New York Times*, June 8, 2016, B1 and B6.
10. Boris Groys, "The Obligation to Self-Design," *e-flux* (November 2008), http://www.e-flux.com/journal/the-obligation-to-self-design/.

Image Captions & Credits

2015. Photo by Angelos Tzortzinis
245T Refugees charge their mobile phones at Keleti railway station in Budapest. Photo by Patrick Witty
245B Businessman using a Motorola DynaTAC 8000X at Meigs Field airport, Chicago, ca. 1984.
246 The Rise of the Cell Phone, graphic by Pooja Saxena
247T X-ray of iPhone
248 Original patent for the Cell phone, 1972
249L President Barack Obama taking a selfie, still from Buzzfeed video, February 2015
249R Two children taking imaginary selfie
254 Refugee's phone protected by balloon on coast of Lesbos, 2015. Photo by Patrick Witty
256 Default profile pictures from different platforms. Image by Weiwei Zhang
258T Original YouTube logo
258B Official screenshots of social media apps on appstore
259 Mark Zuckerberg under map showing Facebook friendship-connections at Mobile World Congress, Barcelona, February 2016
260 People engaged with their phones
261 Kakao Talk friends
262 Woman working in bed
264 Hugh Hefner working in his bed in the Chicago Playboy Mansion, 1966
267 Media equipment integrated into Richard Neutra's bed, VDL House, Los Angeles
268 "Collaborate in Bed," Bluebeam Advertisement
270 Michael Webb, Suitaloon, 1968
271 Metronaps Energy Pod, 2014
272 Edward Snowden in Hong Kong hotel room, still from Citizenfour
1/288 Dancing baby, one of the very first viral gifs

Although we have tried to indicate copyrights as accurately as possible for the images used in this book, it was not possible to contact all of the copyright holders. Interested parties should contact Lars Müller Publishers.

Courtesy Alvar Aalto Archive: 112R. AFP/Getty Images: 124. Albertina, Vienna: 200. Stephen Alvarez/National Geographic Creative: 72. AP: 242. Michael Webb © Archigram 1968: 270. Maxime Aubert: 62. Stiftung Bauhaus Dessau: 133. Lee Roger Berger Research Team: 48. Courtesy TU Braunschweig: 20. Bibliothèques d'Amiens Métropole: 41. Bluebeam: 268. © The British Library Board, 79. University Art Museum, University of California, Santa Barbara: 126. Cambridge University Library: 37. Courtesy Dr. Juan A. de Carlos. Cajal Legacy. Instituto Cajal (CSIC), Madrid: 57. Trustees of Columbia University: 60. Javier DeFelipe: 55. Editorial Domus S.p.A. Milano: 192T. © Eames Office: 100, 117, 118. Al Fenn – The

LIFE Picture Collection/Getty Images: 228L. © FLC/ADAGP, Paris, 2016: 104, 112L, 114, 134, 157, 158T, 158B, 189T, 189B, 190L, 190R, 191T, 194, 195, 196. © FLC / ADAGP, Paris, 2016 and © ADAGP, Paris, 2016: 115. Eileen Gray Archives/Archive of Art & Design Victoria and Albert Museum: 120, 260. Frank and Lillian Gilbreth Collection, Archives Center, Smithsonian Institution: 153. Courtesy Fripp Design and Research: 225. © Estate of George Grosz, Princeton N.J./VG Bild-Kunst, Bonn 2016: 154. B.S. Halpern (T. Hengl; D. Groll) / Wikimedia Commons: 11. © Mia-Jane Harris: 74. © Harvard Art Museums/Busch-Reisinger Museum, Gift of Ati Johanssen, BRGA.1.28: 209. Courtesy Hollein Archives: 140. © Chris Jordan: 14. © Dmitriy Kuzmichev: 28. © 2016 Austrian Frederick and Lillian Kiesler Private Foundation, Vienna: 156, 180. ©1991 Hans Namuth Estate, Courtesy Center for Creative Photography, Collection Austrian Frederick and Lillian Kiesler Private Foundation, Vienna: 176. Lessing/British Museum: 44. Courtesy of the Library of Congress, LC-DIG-pga-0049: 38. Courtesy Patrick Slade: 227B. © Nadya Lukic: 241. © Burt Glinn/Magnum Photos: 264. Paolo Mazzarello: 51. MPK-WTAP: 67. Courtesy NASA Johnson Space Center: 16. NASA/Goddard Space Flight Center: 12, 86. NASA/GSFC/METI/ERSDAC/JAROS, and U.S./Japan ASTER Science Team: 13. U.S. National Institute of Health: 218. Courtesy of the National Library of Medicine: 221, 223. © Tony Law for MetroNaps: 271. © The Trustees of the Natural History Museum, London: 42. Alex Norton, EyeWire: 256. Dimitri Otis/© Getty Images: 35. OMA archives: 168T, 169. University of Oxford, Nuffield department of Clinical Neurosciences: 226B. Courtesy radio-guy.net: 227T. Dr. Gurdeep Sing Ratr: 224T. REUTERS/Albert Gea: 259. Kinez Riza: 64. Courtesy © The Royal Society: 30. © The Bernard Rudofsky Estate/ Bildrecht Vienna 2016: 184, 185. © Satflare.com: 8. Pooja Saxena: 246. © Howard Schatz: 229. Courtesy Smithsonian's Human Origins Program: 68L, 68R. Courtesy Richard Steinmetz, 130. Smithsonian Museum: 224B. M. C. Stiner and S. L. Kuhn: 65. Süleymaniye Library: 56L. Courtesy Politecnico di Torino, sezione Archivi della Biblioteca "Roberto Gabetti," Fondo Carlo Mollino: 191B, 192B. © Sven Torfinn/Panos: 240. Courtesy David Travers / Arts and Architecture: 88. © Bernard Tschumi: 187. Angelos Tzortzinis/AFP Getty images: 244. Peter Cox/Collection Van Abbemuseum, Eindhoven: 213. © VG Bild-Kunst, Bonn 2016: 110, 203, 210, 216. © Achille Weider / Fotostiftung Schweiz: 138, 144. © Wien Museum: 206, 207 © John Wiley & Sons, New York: 159, 160. © Pattrick Witty: 245T, 254.

Beatriz Colomina is Professor of Architecture and Founding Director of the Media and Modernity Program, Princeton University.

Mark Wigley is Professor and Dean Emeritus, Graduate School of Architecture, Planning and Preservation, Columbia University.

—

This book gathers our thoughts when preparing the 3rd Istanbul Design Biennial, ideas that guided the project, grew during it, and go beyond it. Like any design, an exhibition provokes new thoughts in the people that make it, and making is always collaborative. We want to especially thank the IKSV team for being such supportive colleagues over the last year and a half. Evangelos Kotsioris, our assistant curator, was an ever-thoughtful companion. The graduate students in our Fall and Spring classes on "What is Design?" at Princeton and Columbia University were a delight in testing ideas to the limit, as was the joint team of Princeton and Columbia students that worked with us on the Biennial over the summer. Thanks also to Bart-Jan Polman for image research. It was a pleasure to work with Okay Karadayilar on the design. Making a book with Lars Müller and his wonderful team was a real privilege. Special thanks to Elise Jaffe and Jeffrey Brown for their great kindness in supporting this project.

are we human?
notes on an archaeology of design

AUTHORS
Beatriz Colomina, Mark Wigley

COPYEDITING & PROOFREADING
Keonaona Peterson

DESIGN
Okay Karadayılar

COORDINATION
Maya Rüegg

PRINTING & BINDING
Graspo, Zlín, the Czech Republic

PAPER
G-Print 90gr/m^2

TYPEFACES
Anselm Family *by* Storm Type Foundry

Lars Müller Publishers
Zürich, Switzerland
www.lars-mueller-publishers.com

Distributed in North America by ARTBOOK | D.A.P.
www.artbook.com

ISBN 978-3-03778-511-9

Printed in the Czech Republic

Published in collaboration with IKSV (Istanbul Foundation for Culture and Arts)

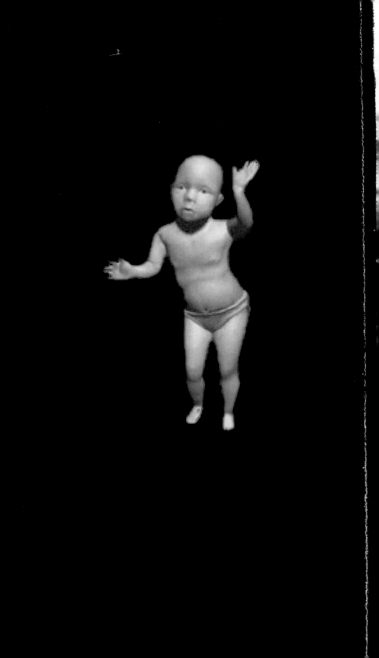